T0353661

Seeking a

Higher

Power

A Guide to the Second Step

"What you seek is seeking you." – Rumi

Michael Cowl Gordon

authorHOUSE®

AuthorHouse™
1663 Liberty Drive
Bloomington, IN 47403
www.authorhouse.com
Phone: 833-262-8899

Published by AuthorHouse 02/25/2025

ISBN: 979-8-8230-4298-7 (sc)
ISBN: 979-8-8230-4297-0 (e)

Library of Congress Control Number: 2025901536

Print information available on the last page.

This book is printed on acid-free paper.

Scripture quotations marked NIV are taken from the Holy Bible, New International Version. NIV*. Copyright © 2011 by International Bible Society. Used by permission of Zondervan. All rights reserved. [Biblica]*

Cover Photo is credited to Rebecca Robinson, or to www.rebecca-robinson.org.

Contents

Acknowledgements vii

Disclaimer ix

How to use this book xi

Introduction xiii

Great Minds and Great Ideas - I

Bill Wilson and Alcoholics Anonymous 1

   Preparation for the search for a higher power 5

      Humility 6

      Surrender 10

      Open-mindedness 12

      Willingness 13

      Courage 15

Great Minds and Great Ideas - II

Joseph Campbell and the Heroic Journey 18

   Character assets needed in the search for a higher power 21

      Honesty 22

      Forgiveness 24

      Gratitude 28

      Compassion 33

      Lovingkindness 36

Great Minds and Great Ideas - III

Rabbi Abraham Joshua Heschel and "Radical Amazement" 37

   Beauty as a gateway to a higher power 41

      Awe and Wonder 42

      Art 45

      Music 47

      Poetry 50

Great Minds and Great Ideas - IV

Carl Jung – Psychology and Spirituality.. 52

    Spirituality – A pathway to a higher power............................... 56

        Love... 60

        Soul 63

        Heart 67

        Connection.. 69

        Meditation.. 72

        Mystery 74

        Mysticism 75

    Religion 76

        Prayer 81

        The Bible and Other Sacred Writings 87

        Creation 89

        Atheism 92

        Agnosticism 95

        Symbols 97

        Heaven and Hell... 102

    Special topics 104

        Native American Spirituality – The Red Road 105

        Buddhism and other Eastern religions........................... 111

        Kabbalah 119

Great Minds and Great Ideas - V

Albert Einstein 124

Great Minds and Great Ideas – VI

Quantum Physics... 127

Conclusion... 131

Appendix A – The God Word in Alcoholics Anonymous
                Literature... 133

Appendix B – Names of God 139

Appendix C – It's the Truth... 149

Appendix D – The Twelve Steps of Alcoholics Anonymous.............. 151

Bibliography.. 153

Suggested Reading... 161

Acknowledgements

I could not have put this project together without a great deal of help. I am grateful to all the people who have put their heart and effort into writing their own works, and to those who have allowed me to quote excerpts from their wise teachings. I also am grateful to the many patients and colleagues from whom I have learned so much, whether they meant to teach me or not. One stands out and should be mentioned, Phil B. from Tennessee, who introduced me to Joseph Campbell and the heroic journey. I was involved in the practice of addiction medicine from 1972 until my retirement in 2023. It was quite a trip. During the same time, I involved myself in twelve-step recovery groups and I continue to derive great benefit from my friends in these groups all over the world. My family has been my primary source of encouragement and support, especially my dear wife, Judy, and my wonderful daughter, Michelle. I should also thank the oncology team at Emory University, Winship Cancer Institute, for keeping me not only alive but well since my diagnosis in 2019. Thanks as well to the Authorhouse team for their support through the publishing process. Finally, I must express my gratitude to my higher power for bringing me into this marvelous universe and allowing me to enjoy it and to be at least somewhat useful and productive.

Disclaimer

Excerpts from Alcoholics Anonymous (AA) materials are reprinted with the permission of Alcoholics Anonymous World Services, Inc. ("AAWS"). Permission to reprint these excerpts does not mean that AAWS has reviewed or approved the contents of this publication, or that AA necessarily agrees with the views expressed herein. AA is a program of recovery from alcoholism *only*—use of the excerpts in connection with programs and activities which are patterned after AA, but which address other problems or in any other non-AA context, does not imply otherwise.

How to use this book

This book is a collection of mostly short essays written for people who are in search of a higher power. I want to be clear that I am not trying to convince anybody of anything. I do hope to provide what could be helpful ideas to think about to assist in the reader's search for a higher power. Predictably, some of the essays will have more interest for some than others. I do not necessarily recommend reading the book straight through from cover to cover, but of course you may find this method most suitable. I suggest that you look at the table of contents and see what essays appeal to your level of interest. In some places the book will seem to be expressing thoughts that force the reader to think more deeply. This will appeal to some more than others.

After many of my short essays I have included writings of others. These are all included to underscore, to clarify, and to add to my own words. For these sections I use the heading, "The Wisdom of Others." I think of myself as a miner of precious gems. As I read books that others have written, I find treasures that I like to share with my readers. After some of the "Wisdom of Others" quotations, I have added a comment of my own. These comments are preceded by my initials, MCG. In a few places I have repeated myself, using the same quotations twice. I justify this by thinking that my readers may well not read the entire book, and that a quote that I use in one place may help me to clarify or emphasize another point that I make elsewhere. Occasionally I will include the suggestion "(see)" in the text. This refers to another topic included in the book that the reader may choose to look at. For example, in the section on meditation the reader will find, "Some people may enjoy listening to music (see) as they walk." This will refer the reader to another section, in this case, the essay on music, for additional context.

Introduction

The impetus for writing this book came to me from my concern over the problem created for many by the directive in the AA program that members seek a higher power in order to recover from alcoholism. Some people may be hostile to the idea of God or may feel indifferent to or disconnected from any sense of God or a higher power. My hope here is to make this idea more approachable. I ask my readers to be open-minded and willing to consider ideas that either they never thought of before, or ideas which they have rejected previously. My target audience is primarily newcomers to twelve-step recovery, especially people who are troubled by the higher power idea or resistant to it. I hope that others can benefit as well. AA talks about "God as you understand Him" and says people can use their own idea about God or a higher power. For most, this by itself is good but not helpful enough. My purpose here is to give some guidance for such people who are trying find a way to accept the suggestion of seeking a higher power in order to recover from their addiction, whatever it might be. In many of the essays I talk about God. I hope this does not turn the reader off. My goal is to help people expand their minds to consider new ways of thinking about God, or about a higher power. The problem is usually not that people believe that there is no God, although for some this is the case. It is rather that people don't really know what to think about God or the idea of God.

We can hardly deal with the topic of searching for a higher power without talking about God, but I want to be clear that the emphasis here is on the search. The search is a process, a journey, and it will lead to wherever it leads. Again, it will help the searcher to be open-minded. What I hear from a great many people is, "I believe in something, but I can't say exactly what." This might even be the majority position, certainly much more common than people who call themselves atheists. Atheists will readily acknowledge that their own power has its limits, and that there are forces in the world much more powerful than they are. One can easily provide evidence that show the presence of forces that are real, yet invisible to the naked eye. Magnetic fields are a good example. A powerful magnet might look like an ordinary piece of metal but put it under a sheet of paper and shake iron filings on the paper, and you will observe the filings line up along the force lines of the magnet. Albert Einstein intuited that mass and energy are interchangeable, that within a mass object there is an astounding amount of force being held, an amount of power almost beyond imagination. So, within the physical, observable world there are fields and forces beyond what we might expect or imagine.

Let's deal with "the God word" problem for a moment. When I say "God" in these pages, what am I referring to? For that matter, whenever anyone in our society says "God," what are they talking about? If we can't communicate clearly then much of our effort is wasted. On the one hand, most philosophers and theologists agree that God is ultimately unknowable. We lack the capacity to even think about God as God really is. On the other hand, I think everyone knows generally what we mean when we say God, at least in the West. According to common understanding in the world in which I live, it is God who created the world, who listens to our prayers, who responds to them in some way, who cares about us personally, who blesses America or wherever we live, who presides over a spiritual realm called heaven where we receive our rewards after we die, who expects a standard of good behavior, and who wants to be loved and obeyed. In other words, He is the Big Guy in the Sky, Large and In-Charge. Yet, it is precisely this idea of God that so many people find unacceptable. My entire purpose with this book is to help my readers find other ways to think about a higher power—especially, people for whom addiction has become a problem in which their well-being has become seriously threatened.

When people develop addictions, whether to substances or behaviors, they are robbed of their quality of life as the addiction eats away at health, mental and emotional stability, self-esteem, and social structure. Left unchecked, the addict is at risk of disability, incarceration, bankruptcy of every description, and even premature death. For an alcoholic, getting sobered up turns out to be almost impossible without outside help, and being open to outside help usually doesn't happen until he reaches a stage of desperation. Once open to help, the addict may experience multiple failed attempts to arrest the addiction. Even involvement with Alcoholics Anonymous, a program that can claim over two million recoveries, by itself fails at first more often than it succeeds. (Note: In this book I use the terms "addict" and "alcoholic" interchangeably. I hope this doesn't bother anyone. Also, I tried not to get tied up in knots over the use of pronouns. If this is a problem for some readers, I understand, but I am going for readability.)

It is worthwhile considering the reasons that AA may not work for those people who fail to find recovery within its rooms. For one thing, many people never even try AA as a solution to their addiction. Reasons for this include the remarkable capacity for suffering that some people have. Denial, the psychological defense mechanism which prevents people from seeing the painful realities in their lives, can certainly prevent people from taking appropriate action to correct a problem. If the problem is not seen as it actually is, then the solution applied to it will not work. This can go on for years, or for the lifetime of the addict. If the problem is never recognized for what it is, nothing constructive will be done about it. The alcoholic may be forced into treatment by family, employers, or the law, but the treatment won't take if the alcoholic does not see that what he is learning about applies to him.

But let us say that we are past this stage of denial, and the addict is acknowledging a problem and looking for answers. He is no longer blaming anything outside of himself for the addictive behaviors. It is no longer the husband, the wife, the kids, the bills, the boss, or the in-laws. As Walt Kelly had his loveable character, Pogo, say one day after venturing into the swamp, "We have met the enemy, and he is us." Let's suppose that the alcoholic has been advised to go to AA to find the solution to his problem. Now, what can go wrong? Well, again, he may refuse to go. He (or she) may believe that AA is a religious organization, or worse, a cult. He may think that he will find himself in a group of people with a lower social standing, or people who won't understand him. He may be embarrassed or ashamed to associate with AA. Or he may still think he can stay sober on his own, or with the help of friends and family, or his church. Of course, some people do find a path to sobriety without AA. But very few of them do it entirely "on their own." And experience has shown that most people who do quit on their own fail to find inner contentment or happiness. The underlying personality factors that propelled the addiction remain unremedied.

Another potential obstacle to finding success through AA is the requirement that the person must find a higher power upon which to rely. Of those people who walk into (or log into) an AA meeting for the first time, at least half are not on good terms with a higher power. What has God done for them thus far in their lives? At the times when they have prayed, did their prayers get answered? Every day people are hungry, unsheltered, and abused, and most of them pray. Doesn't God allow children to get cancer? And generally, people who are told they need to find a higher power assume that we are talking about God. This assumption is reinforced as one looks around the room at the slogans and AA steps and traditions hanging on the walls with the word God sprinkled upon them liberally. And a quick perusal of the group's literature will find the God word frequently used. (See Appendix A.) *It is this person, sitting in this chair, confronted by this situation, whom I hope to reach with this book.* After reading this book the reader may not know any more about who or what God is than when they started but hopefully will have had a chance to consider some ideas they had not considered previously. Rabbi Harold Kushner wrote that "Religion is not first and foremost a series of teachings about God. Religion is first and foremost the community through which you learn to understand the world and grow to be human."[1] This tells me that the search for a higher power is best and most effectively conducted within a community of seekers. Clergyman and social activist Willian Sloane Coffin wrote, "We can build a community out of seekers of truth, but not of possessors of truth."[2] This really is a book about a search rather than a book about The Truth. (See Appendix C.) My belief is that people who honestly engage in this search will find enough of what they are seeking to meet their recovery needs.

---

[1] Harold Kushner, *Who Needs God?* Pocket Books, 194.
[2] Ibid., 191.

It may be worthwhile to explore what leads people to think about a higher power's existence in the world. Such speculation can begin by considering the beauty we find around us. Whereas to a certain extent beauty really is in the eye of the beholder, there are certain things in which agreement can be generally found. Such things as a sunrise or sunset, a flower, a rolling cultivated landscape, a baby's toes, all inspire a sense of admiration and a pleasing sense within our being. Gazing upon such beauty gives rise to wonder. We are inspired to wonder how such a lovely, beautiful, and marvelous thing can be so sublime. The experience of wonder can naturally result in a sense of awe, as the mind tries to embrace what kind of power can produce such beauty. At times it is enough to simply embrace the beauty. Indeed, one of the ways in which we can connect with the universe is just in this way. We gaze upon the star-filled sky on a cloudless night, and especially if the area is unpolluted by city light, the sight is breathtaking. But how can we gaze into the unfathomable expanse without wondering about the universe? How vast is it? Where did it come from? What does it mean? At such times people in their "radical amazement," as Rabbi Abraham Joshua Heschel calls it, think about the kind of power that could produce such a cosmic, beautiful reality. In writing about wonder and awe in his book, *God in Search of Man*, Heschel says, "Awareness of the divine begins in wonder" [3].

Beyond beauty, immensity, wonder and thus awe we may be inspired by the unexpected appearance of order in the universe. An example of this is within the plant world, where the arrangement of petals, fruit sprouts, and such things as pinecone bracts follow the mathematical regularity known as the Fibonacci sequence. The Fibonacci sequence is a series of numbers in which the next number in the sequence is the sum of the two preceding numbers. Thus, the sequence is 0, 1, 1, 2, 3, 5, 8, 13, 21, 34, 55, and so on. If one were to count the number of petals in a flower (say, a sunflower) in which the petals are arranged in ever-enlarging concentric circles, it would be found that as the flower enlarges the number of petals in each next-largest circle follows the Fibonacci sequence exactly. And this is only one example of the order found in the universe. So, the universe

[3] Abraham Joshua Heschel, *God in Search of Man: A Philosophy of Judaism*, Farrar, Straus, and Giroux, 1955, 46.

not only is large and filled with beauty, but its arrangement shows definite signs of order.

Most people when they contemplate the world conclude that there must be some creative force which has caused the world to be. Of course, there are many who are willing to accept the proposition the this is not the case, that the world simply is. Here is one of the many places where I encourage the reader to draw his own conclusions and have his own opinions. I am not trying to convince anyone of anything. I am trying to open the reader's mind to think about things that they may not have considered before or that deserve to be reconsidered now. After all, while some readers may have picked up this book out of curiosity, many readers will have reached a point in their lives where things are going very badly for them, and for whom a new understanding of themselves and the world they live in might put them on a better footing. Many such people have found their way to a twelve-step group, where they are told they need to seek a higher power which will help them get to a better place in their lives.

People often find it difficult to believe in a God who is "personally" involved with the world and loves us because of the obvious presence of evil and suffering. Much has already been written on this problem, and I will not summarize all the arguments that attempt to reconcile this conundrum. They literally fill books and have occupied the efforts of philosophers and theologians for thousands of years. The word which is applied to the study of why God permits evil in the world is theodicy.

One way of explaining the presence of evil and suffering has to do with man's free will. People can choose to be good or bad, selfish or generous, loving or hateful, forgiving or vengeful. If there is a God that created the world and set people in it, this God must have had a reason. Without my having any inside information on this, I will suggest two possibilities, at the same time admitting that since God is incomprehensible, I have no way of knowing what God had in mind (nor does anyone else). But still, we can try to make sense out of the world we live in.

Possibility number one has to do with the commonly held belief that God is Love. Should God be Infinite Loving Energy, as imagined, then where is the love object to which this loving energy can be directed? I find it unimaginable that such a mass of love-energy could exist without having a love object—thus, the universe. Possibility number two is related to the first situation. If we postulate that God is Love, then we must acknowledge that God is possessed of feelings. Proceeding on this assumption, I can imagine God alone in the universe with nobody to have a relationship with. James Weldon Johnson in his poem *The Creation*, opens with the following verses:

> *"And God stepped out on space,*
> *And he looked around and said:*
> *I'm lonely—*
> *I'll make me a world.*[4]

If God created a world so that He could have relationships, then God's will for us is to acknowledge His existence and respond to Him, hopefully by returning the loving feelings that are directed towards us. It would be meaningless to God if the only reason we love God and take good care of the world is because we have no choice in the matter. Thus, we have free will. It doesn't make it any easier that God's nature and even existence is shrouded in mystery. Very few people in recorded history have had the experience of God speaking directly to them in their native language. The Bible records such instances, but the Bible in the view of many, myself included, leaves much to be desired as a historical document.

I suppose I just offended some people. This was not my intention. I assume that my readers are searching for a higher power. Those who are reading these pages and who also take the Bible as the literal actual Word of God, in their minds have already found their higher power, or so it would seem. I simply am trying to respectfully point people to seek and hopefully find a higher power who is not found in a religious system or theology that they have found impossible to accept for themselves. I

---

[4] James Weldon Johnson, *God's Trombones: Seven Negro Sermons in Verse*, Viking Press, 1927, 15.

believe that there is a great deal of value in reading the Bible (see) as part of that search, but not everyone is going to find all the Bible's claims and statements believable.

There is no doubt that a group of individuals can accomplish more than individuals working on their own, even if we are talking about the same people. There is a dynamic within a group that has its own power. Some of this can certainly be at the intellectual level, as when people "put their heads together" to solve a problem. It can also occur at an emotional level as may be seen in such events as group therapy or religious worship services. Finally, it can be experienced at the level of the heart, where people can connect with each other in love. It is my belief that all three are in operation in the twelve-step programs. People seeking relief from a serious enough life problem that they reach out to a twelve-step program have felt a serious sense of defeat in their lives. They have become demoralized, isolated, self-hating, and angry. Having arrived at the program, they are told that there is hope, that many others have succeeded at recovery, and that to recover what they need to do is become connected to the program. While they are told that they need a higher power, they are also told not to worry about that now. Just go to meetings, don't drink, drug, gamble (or whatever) one day at a time, get a sponsor, and start working on the steps. A higher power is already at work because the newcomer is developing a sense of connection to other human beings, connection itself being one of the highest powers in existence. He is told not to worry about "the God stuff" right now. Soon he knows others, and they know him by name. He receives encouragement, hears the wisdom of the program, starts to experience a lessening of his obsessions and compulsions, and begins to have hope. This is all the higher power he needs at this point, and the truth is that for some, the power of connection with the group may be all the higher power they ever need. As one travels the path of twelve-step recovery, one may develop ideas about a higher power that go beyond one's initial connection with the group. All one needs is to be open to whatever comes their way in the spiritual domain.

Bill Wilson and Alcoholics Anonymous

Alcoholics Anonymous developed out of a meeting between William Griffith Wilson, a New York Wall Street businessman, and Robert Holbrook Smith, an Akron, Ohio colon and rectal surgeon. Both men were severely alcoholic and had tried to quit drinking unsuccessfully for years. Wilson at the time of the meeting had been abstinent for five months, having had what he termed a spiritual experience while in a detox center. He was so enthused with his transformation that he thought that if he shared it with others then they too would be able to quit drinking. He went further, imagining that these people would share their experience with still others, initiating a chain reaction resulting in the recovery of millions of alcoholics. For a five-month period he went into bars and detox centers talking with other alcoholics, but the only alcoholic sober after all this effort was himself.

After discussing his failure to convert anyone with his doctor, William Silkworth, he took the doctor's suggestion that he hold off on pressing the spiritual angle when talking with others. Instead, he should begin by explaining the nature of the alcoholic's disease which Silkworth termed "an allergy combined with a mental obsession." Only after interesting the man in this idea should Wilson bring up the spiritual approach to recovery. The first time Wilson tried this approach was with Bob Smith. Wilson was in Akron on a business trip, and when the deal fell through, he wanted to drink. Instead, he contacted a clergyman who put him in touch with an Oxford Group member, Harriet Seiberling. The Oxford Group was the organization that Wilson had affiliated himself with during this five-month period of sobriety. It was a lay group of Christians who were trying

1

to live their lives based upon spiritual principles. Smith had been going to Oxford Group meetings in Akron for over two years but had failed to make any headway with his drinking. After much persuasion from his wife, Smith agreed to meet with the man from New York, but only for fifteen minutes, expecting to get another lecture on the evils of drink. Instead, he stayed talking with Wilson for six hours. He stopped drinking immediately but relapsed briefly several weeks later. His last drink was thought to be June 10, 1935, which is taken as the date of the founding of Alcoholics Anonymous. By this early date one of the cardinal principles of recovery had already been discovered— that of not drinking one day at a time. Newcomers were told that all they had to do was not drink today, and that "almost anyone can stop drinking for one day." This remains fundamental to the program today.

Later that summer Wilson returned to New York City where he slowly gathered together a group of men who had quit drinking using his method. In 1937 he disassociated his group from the Oxford Group and began to write a book describing the nature of alcoholism, as well as his solution to the problem. Meanwhile, Smith continued to work with alcoholics in Akron. As word spread, a great many were referred to Akron for detox and treatment under Smith's guidance. He estimated that he had worked with around five thousand alcoholics over the next fifteen years, never accepting payment for his services. The Akron group disaffiliated from the Oxford Group in 1939, the same year that the book, *Alcoholics Anonymous*, was published. The group drew its name from the title of the book, which subsequently has been nicknamed the Big Book by AA members. Both men endured severe financial hardship in the early years, and both received admirable encouragement and support from their wives. The program grew slowly, groups popping up in cities around the country as newly sober men carried the Big Book with them and recruited newcomers. In 1941 Jack Alexander wrote an article in the Saturday Evening Post, giving AA a national audience. Thousands of inquiries came into New York, and Alcoholics Anonymous was on its way.

At that time, though, Wilson faced a new kind of problem. Other temperance societies had sprung up before, some of them attracting tens of thousands or more, but none had lasted. Bill Wilson was determined that AA would grow and endure whatever challenges it may face. By far, the greatest challenge was internal dissention among the members, some of whom had raging egos that demanded attention and control. Wilson was aware that he possessed a measure of these traits himself. If an issue was important enough to him, he would sometimes push too hard and alienate others, but things always seemed to settle down. Wilson tried to base his actions on the principles of honesty, prayerfulness, humility, compassion, and being useful, and he wrote extensively on these topics.

The program of Alcoholics Anonymous was based on twelve steps to recovery. The first step involved admitting defeat, which for many if not most was the hardest step of all. The next step involved coming to believe in a higher power that could assist with recovery. Here was another problem for many, because Bill Wilson, Bob Smith, and many others called this higher power God, and about half of the people they encountered had an issue with the idea of God, let alone with reliance on God. This issue was somewhat resolved by adding the words "as you understand Him," after the word God. At this point the next step was a step of surrender to a higher power, involving a decision to place one's will and life into the hands of this higher power. The reluctance of newcomers to take this leap of faith was tempered by the fact that it seemed to be working for the sober people they were meeting, people who gave no hint of being religious fanatics. From this point the steps carry one through a process of self-examination, self-improvement, character-building, and repaying wherever possible the debts of the past, financial and otherwise. Finally, the member is expected to practice daily self-awareness, spiritual awareness, the helping of other alcoholics, and to be the best person he can be that day.

Bill Wilson's belief about the structure of Alcoholics Anonymous was that it should have as little structure as possible. Leaders were to have no authority. Decisions were to be made by the conscience of the group, which hopefully would be guided by a "loving God." During the 1940's he devoted most of his energy to developing and implementing these guidelines, which were officially adopted at the first international convention of Alcoholics Anonymous in 1950 as the Twelve Traditions. We can safely say that the

3

Twelve Steps and Twelve Traditions have passed the test of time after almost 90 years since Bill and Bob first met at Harriett Seiberling's coach house. Bill Wilson received many honors and would have received many more had he been willing to accept them. Anonymity is an important tradition in AA. Nobody, not even Bill Wilson, could speak for AA. This tradition, like most of the others, was learned by trial and error. Two honors, though, are worth mentioning here. Time magazine listed Bill Wilson as one of the 100 most influential people of the twentieth century. And writer and philosopher Aldous Huxley said of Bill that he was the greatest social architect of the twentieth century. There can be no denying that the twelve-step approach to recovery has been a great success. It has been successfully adapted to over one hundred different problems leading millions of people to the recovery of their lives. And while it is difficult to say how many members there are in Alcoholics Anonymous because there are no dues, attendance rolls, or membership lists, we can easily say that millions have had quality, sober lives because of their involvement with AA.

Preparation for the search for a higher power

Before we begin the actual search for a higher power it is important to prepare ourselves for the journey. Here I emphasize five domains of personality that, if developed, will enhance the likelihood of success. They are humility, surrender, open-mindedness, willingness, and courage. All are ideals—none can be accomplished absolutely; but we should understand that we should strive to work for as much as we are able of these assets and to recognize their value in our lives.

Humility

There are certain preconditions to establish prior to embarking on a legitimate search for a higher power. It should be obvious that if we must seek a higher power, we must not yet have a clear understanding of that which we seek. Therefore, we don't know everything. More to the point, we also don't know everything that we need to know to live successfully. This has become a big problem, and we are at the point of admitting this to ourselves. Everyone acquires certain beliefs and principles upon which they establish their lives. Even though one's life may be in disarray, many people nevertheless hold certain "truths" to be inviolate. For example, such beliefs may include not trusting anyone or anything outside of oneself. One of the hardest things to do is to challenge and re-examine these fundamental "truths," but at certain times we must do so, and typically the time when this is most needed is when we have lost our grip, and our lives have gone off the rails.

My suggestions to people in need of a major upgrade in the quality of their lives is to resign from the position of being the smartest person in the room, be serious about learning what they may have contributed to their own troubles, and to be open to change their mind about any idea of theirs that is not working. An idea is not working if it is blocking progress on their life's journey and keeping them stuck in the misery of yesterday. The transition from being sure of yourself, to questioning yourself, and to finding a new way often involves traveling in darkness for a long time, and we must have humility combined with at least some hope of success. Upon consideration of the possibility of attending AA, many people will agree to at least try it, but don't want to have to buy any of the "God stuff." Again, it helps to receive encouragement from those who have already traveled this path. This assumes, of course, that the first step has been taken: we have admitted defeat. If we acknowledge hitting bottom, that we can't tolerate further suffering and self-degradation, then we become open to deflation of the grandiose ego, and the opening of ourselves to humility.

In the process of ego deflation, we acknowledge that we are not all-powerful—we are forced to give up our infantile stance of omnipotence. As we continue to exert effort on our own behalf, we admit that without a higher power we will fail. The teaching of many great spiritual leaders including St. Ignatius of Loyola endorse the dictum that we should work as though everything depends upon ourselves and pray as though everything depends on God. It's a spiritual paradox that the more successful we feel in this program, the more convinced we are that it is not our doing. Our success depends on our higher power. None of us can say, "I did it." As the quality of our life improves, though - as we grow calmer and more self-assured - it is only natural for us to feel we've done something right. We most assuredly have done something right if we are working the twelve steps of this program, for it is a stairway to communion with our higher power, a stairway to serenity. The more time we spend on the steps, the more time we spend with our higher power. It's that simple. So, it is true that we work for our own success, and it is just as true that the success of recovery comes from reliance on our higher power. My success depends on the effort I make in putting myself in the hands of my higher power, or as some say, "my highest power."

Many great spiritual thinkers and theologians have written about humility. There is enough quality material to fill several volumes. The quotes that I include here are a few of those that specifically address the seeking of a higher power.

The Wisdom of Others

Twelve Steps and Twelve Traditions

"Humility and intellect could be compatible, provided we placed humility first. When we began to do that, we received the gift of faith, a faith which works."[5]

"This lack of anchorage to any permanent values, this blindness to the true purpose of our lives, produced another bad result. For just so long as we were convinced that we could live exclusively by our own individual strength and intelligence, for just that long was a working faith in a higher power impossible. This was true even when we believed that God

---

[5] *Twelve Steps and Twelve Traditions*, Alcoholics Anonymous World Services, Inc., 1952, 30.

existed. We could actually have earnest religious beliefs which remained barren because we were still trying to play God ourselves. As long as we placed self-reliance first, a genuine reliance on a higher power was out of the question. That basic ingredient of all humility, a desire to seek and do God's will, was missing."[6]

"During this process of learning more about humility, the most profound result of all was the change in our attitude toward God. And this was true whether we had been believers or unbelievers. We began to get over the idea that God was a sort of bush-league pinch hitter, to be called upon only in an emergency."[7]

"A great turning point in our lives came when we sought for humility as something we really wanted rather than as something we *must* have."[8]

David E. Schoen

"Kierkegaard says that 'it takes humility to take a leap of faith, for the leap is beyond rational control.' Giving up ego control is the biggest leap of faith I can imagine."[9]

Martin Buber

"'In him who is full of himself there is no room for God.' "[10]

---

[6] Ibid., 72.
[7] Ibid., 75.
[8] Ibid., 75.
[9] David E Schoen, *The War of the Gods in Addiction: C.G. Jung, Alcoholics Anonymous, and Archetypal Evil,* Spring Journal Books, 2009, 109.
[10] Martin Buber, *Hasidism and Modern Man,* Humanities Press International, Inc., 1958, 1988, 106.

Andy F.

"In the absence of a belief in God, humility itself is the power greater than ourselves that helps with the removal of our shortcomings."[11]

Rabbi Moshe Chaim Luzzatto (1707 – 1746)

"The essence of humility is in a person's not attaching importance to himself for any reason whatsoever." [12]

---

[11] Andy F, *The Twelve Steps for Agnostics,* 230.
[12] Alan Morinis, *Every Day, Holy Day: 365 Days of Teachings and Practices from the Jewish Tradition of Mussar,* Trumpeter, 2010, 239.

Surrender

With the first of the twelve steps we admit defeat—that we are powerless over our addiction and that our lives have become unmanageable. This does not necessarily equate with surrender. We can admit to loss of control but hold on to the idea that we can still "figure it out." Somehow, someway, we may hope to regain control once we find the elusive secret. Surrender happens only when all hope of regaining control is relinquished. Then, and only then, will the alcoholic wave the white flag of surrender. According to Dr. Harry Tiebout, a psychiatrist who was a very early AA supporter, the obstacle to surrender is the infantile ego—that aspect of the personality that claims absolute authority from the position of the center of the universe. It is "King Baby," sitting in his highchair screaming and banging the tray with his spoon. As Bill Wilson says at the very beginning of *Twelve Steps and Twelve Traditions*, "Who cares to admit complete defeat?"[13] Nobody will seek a higher power if they imagine themselves to be the highest power in their lives. So, the action step involved here is to admit to complete defeat followed by an agreement to seek a power that is greater than themselves—a higher power. Surrender must be total and unconditional. Without reinforcement by going to AA meetings and engaging with the fellowship and a sponsor, it is easy to slip back into denial, nourish the delusion that it wasn't really that bad, that we overreacted in a weak moment, and then retake control. Julius Caesar said, "I came, I saw, I conquered." The alcoholic must say, "I came, I saw, I surrendered."

As Bill Wilson pursued his understanding of what had happened to him at the spiritual level when his obsession with alcohol was removed, he was given a book by psychologist William James, *The Varieties of Religious Experience*. In that book we find James declaring that "Self-surrender has been and always must be regarded as the vital turning point of the religious life."[14] Surrender is widely recognized as a critical step in the heroic journey of resurrecting one's life from a self-destructive path. The more we are filled with our sense of our own power, the less room there is and the less need

[13] *Twelve Steps and Twelve Traditions*, 21.
[14] William James, *The Varieties of Religious Experience*, First Modern Library Edition, 1936, 209.

there is for a higher power. When we finally realize that we are powerless, we hopefully will be willing to let go of the lifestyle and beliefs that failed us and be open to new ideas and practices. Saying this another way, we must give up control and stop playing God. Only after surrendering can our search begin. The main thing we must believe at this point is that whatever we thought we knew, it wasn't helping. Indeed, the disaster that our life had become was mired in and was in part the responsibility of our best thinking.

The Wisdom of Others

Harold Kushner

"The ... wrong turn from which so many subsequent mistakes and problems follow, is not disobedience or lust, but the arrogant claim of self-sufficiency, that idea that we don't need help, that we are strong enough to do it entirely on our own."[15]

William Alexander

"So, when 'I' gave up, what really happened? I surrendered. Surrender has been described variously as a functional acceptance of reality on an unconscious level, a huge emotional displacement or rearrangement, or a miracle" .... For me, surrender as a miracle was this: *Rather than me changing my mind, my mind changed.* And, in order for this to happen, I had to let go of the pride that was choking the life right out of me." (emphasis mine)[16].

---

[15] *Who Needs God?*, 183.
[16] William Alexander, *Ordinary Recovery: Mindfulness, Addiction, and the Path of Lifelong Sobriety,* Shambala, 2010, 32.

Open-mindedness

Having taken the first step, having admitted that our best efforts at gaining control of our lives had failed us, we are forced to admit to ourselves that if we are to resolve our difficulties, we must find a new source of help. In AA the new source of help, according to the second step, is suggested to be a higher power. Since we have exhausted our own supply of ideas on what to do to salvage our lives, a suggestion to try anything at all must be considered. That the suggestion to come to a reliance on a higher power may seem to be odd, unwelcome, or disagreeable, is beside the point. We must be willing to try anything. Fortunately, if we have wound up in a twelve-step group, we are not falling in with a bunch of lunatics. These are people who are utilizing a proven system of recovery. The fact that the system seems to us to be unlikely to work is not a good enough reason to close our minds to it. Our own ideas have failed us. We don't need to understand how this suggestion might start us off in the right direction. "Figuring it out" is not a step on the road to recovery. If we have pneumonia, and an antibiotic is prescribed, we don't need to understand how the antibiotic kills the bacteria in our lungs. We just need to trust the physician who has had years of education and training in the treatment of infectious diseases and proceed to take the antibiotic. A wholesale change in attitude is required. We must become teachable. Such a desire to learn how to live differently will place us firmly on the road to recovery. We may come to understand eventually why the suggestion to seek a higher power was effective, but this is of no significance to us now. If we are open-minded enough to let go of "our old ideas"[17] to make room for new ones, then we will be successful in being restored to a better life, typically a better life than we had imagined was possible.

---

[17] *Alcoholics Anonymous, The Story of How Many Thousands of Men and Women Have Recovered from Alcoholism,* Alcoholics Anonymous World Services, Inc. 4th ed., 2001, 58.

Willingness

People who lack a belief in a higher power may not be aware of their internal resistance to such a belief. They think that they do not believe in a higher power, or if you will, God, for good reasons such as it makes no sense to them, or that if God was so powerful why doesn't God prevent bad things from happening? There they stop, and don't consider what they would be giving up if they became willing to believe in a power greater than themselves. It's not only that they need to change their minds, but that *they need to lay the groundwork for changing their minds.* The chief obstacle is pride. A person must be able to admit that he might have been wrong about a fundamental and deeply held belief. Ego deflation at depth is the desired goal for the alcoholic to experience to stop playing God and to become willing to believe in a higher power. It is not possible to win this game until we lose the battle with alcohol without any question or equivocation. Once defeat is total, the alcoholic is open to a suggestion to try the AA method of recovery; and this journey begins with seeking a higher power. And it eventually becomes apparent to the seeker that it is the seeking itself, the journey itself, that is the achievement. There is no end game in the search.

The Wisdom of Others

Grapevine Word for the Day, April 20, 2024

"I was relieved to learn that I didn't have to believe, only be willing to believe. This I could do."[18]

---

[18] Grapevine Word for the Day, April 20, 2024, *From Make Believe to Belief,* Charleston, West Virginia, June 1981, from *Voices of Long-Term Sobriety: Oldtimers Stories from AA,* AA Grapevine, 2009.

Michael Cowl Gordon

Abraham Joshua Heschel

"All that is left to us is a choice—to answer or to refuse to answer. Yet the more deeply we listen, the more we become stripped of the arrogance and callousness which alone would enable us to refuse."[19]

Emmet Fox was an ordained minister and a leader in the New Thought movement during the first half of the twentieth century. He led the Divine Science Church of the Healing Christ, authored several books and pamphlets, and lectured to large audiences in New York City including at Carnegie Hall. His teaching had a positive influence on Bill Wilson and the early AA members, some of whom would attend his lectures.

Emmet Fox

"To be poor in spirit means to have emptied yourself of all desire to exercise personal self-will, and what is just as important, to have renounced all pre-conceived opinions in the wholehearted search for God. It means to be willing to set aside your present habits of thought, your present views and prejudices, your present way of life if necessary; to jettison, in fact, anything and everything that can stand in your way of your finding God."[20]

---

[19] *God in Search of Man,* 112.
[20] Emmet Fox, *The Sermon on the Mount,* HarperSanFrancisco, 1934, 1935, 1938, 21.

Courage

Courage is a characteristic called for in response to a sense of fear. Fear arises in response to perceived danger, and as such it is a basic human emotion, necessary for survival. It is part of the average person's daily life. For example, nobody can safely drive a car without an awareness of potential danger. As we grow, ideally, we learn how to manage our lives so that fear is a useful tool. More often though, in our complicated lives fear becomes a problem in itself, resulting in needless worry and anxiety. Often, we learn to be distrustful because people who are supposed to take care of us (parents, coaches, teachers, clergy) may prove to be unreliable or even perpetrators of deceit and harm. We also are told about God as we grow. God is supposed to be the ultimate provider of support, safety, and love.

If people let us down, maybe we can cope with this, depending, of course, on the situation. What are we supposed to make, though, of a God who we are told is all-powerful and loves us perfectly but seems indifferent to our disappointments, pain, and suffering? It is a problem that I am sure has existed ever since humans walked on the earth with the capacity to wonder about such things. As we become disillusioned, cynical and bitter, these reactions lead to a loss of faith on the one hand, or even a hatred of God on the other.

In the Big Book of *Alcoholics Anonymous*, Bill Wilson wrote that about half of the original membership were either agnostic or atheists.[21] He also stated that the purpose of the Big Book was to help people find a higher power in order solve their alcohol problem.[22] Given the success of Alcoholics Anonymous in restoring people's lives, then, one solution to finding a higher power would be to read the Big Book. I can completely agree with this plan. But it may not be so simple, or at least, not so easy. The newcomer is told he must give up his old ideas, to let go absolutely.[23] He is told he must be thorough and fearless.[24] So, courage is called for.

---

[21] *Alcoholics Anonymous*, 44.
[22] Ibid., 45.
[23] Ibid., 58.
[24] Ibid., 58.

It is inescapable that the sufferer must be willing to change his attitudes, thoughts, and beliefs, especially about a higher power, and venture into new territory. He must be willing to give up his miserable life with little idea of what he can expect his new life to be. While he is miserable as an active alcoholic, and likely is deeply mired in resentment and self-pity, the prospect of trying a new way of thinking is intimidating. It seems that people can get used to almost anything. However they are living, life may have developed a certain level of comfort. Many homeless people would rather sleep outside in below freezing weather than go to a shelter. There may be great resistance to change. In the heroic journey the hero is called upon to embark on a task that seems impossible to achieve. His first response is to refuse the call to adventure. This is where the alcoholic finds himself when he reaches the rooms of Alcoholics Anonymous. He has come to believe that he cannot quit drinking on his own, but at AA they tell him that he needs to rely on a higher power. And they probably will use the God word. His first reaction, in at least half the cases, will be to resist.

Can he trust these people? They seem to be doing a lot better than he is, and they claim to be alcoholics themselves. The difference is that they don't drink. It is largely from the experience of being with these sober alcoholics and listening to their stories that he finds the courage he needs to try the program, even if he is advised to seek a higher power. This is God as a Group Of Drunks—unquestionably a higher power. The first step in a heroic journey is always the hardest. It may call for an act of desperation, a step that will lead who knows where? From somewhere deep inside there is a scrap of courage to hold onto life and try to do things differently. A key to trying this is having been told he only must do it today. This may make the project seem to be less overwhelming. The heroic journey of recovery will demand courage, but those who try it will discover they are capable of far more than they ever thought possible if they don't try to go it alone. The alcoholic is promised that his higher power will meet him more than halfway, but that he must take that first step. As O. Hobart Mowrer wrote, "Only you can do it, but you can't do it alone."[25]

---

[25] O. Hobart Mowrer, *"Small Groups in Historical Perspective,"* in *Explorations in Self-Help and Mutual Aid*, ed. Leonard D. Borman, Center for Urban Studies, Northwestern University, 1974, 47.

The Wisdom of Others

Susan Jeffers

"We cannot escape fear. We can only transform it into a companion that accompanies us on all our exciting adventures."[26]

Andre Gide

"Man cannot discover new oceans unless he has the courage to lose sight of the shore."[27]

---

[26] Susan Jeffers, https:// azquotes.com>author>20458-susan_jeffers, Top 25 Quotes by Susan Jeffers.
[27] https://www.brainyquote.com/authors/andre-gide-quotes.

Joseph Campbell and the Heroic Journey

Joseph Campbell was a philosopher, educator, and mythologist whose ideas have had a significant effect on the way we think about life. He was born in New York in 1904, and he died in Hawaii in 1987. He was drawn to the study of the mythologies of tribes, religions, and cultures all over the world, and his most notable insight was the similarities of the stories. He observed that cultures that could not possibly have had contact with one another had identical themes in their stories. This suggested to him that the origin of these themes was at a preconscious level that must be carried genetically. Supporting this idea was the work of Dr. Carl Jung (see), the Swiss psychiatrist who developed the theories of the collective unconscious and of archetypes.

A major type of myth, or story that Campbell identified in this regard, was the myth of the hero. He found a striking similarity in the stories of a hero early in the founding of a society, a man or woman who established the safety or dominance of a society in their homeland. Such heroes were often semi-divine, had miraculous birth events, and had superpowers that enabled them to succeed in their endeavors. They usually received their power from the gods who looked with favor upon the heroes and their people. In 1949 Campbell published *The Hero with a Thousand Faces*, a book that established him as a thought leader in the twentieth century. He taught at Sarah Lawrence College for many years and wrote books, mostly about mythology. In 1983 he was interviewed by Bill Moyers at George Lucas' Skywalker ranch. Lucas had been profoundly affected by Campbell's ideas and wrote and produced the Star Wars movies based on the idea of the heroic journey. These interviews were produced as a set of six CDs and a book, both called *The Power of Myth*. *The Power of Myth* was viewed by millions of people, and together with the enormous popularity of Star Wars, firmly established the heroic journey in the consciousness of people all over the world.

I published a book in 2023, *The Twelve Step Pathway: A Heroic Journey of Recovery,* as the first in-depth study of addiction recovery as a heroic journey. I hope that as this book gets more widely read the idea of recovery as a heroic journey will become better established in the world of addiction treatment and recovery, and that others will take up the study and write their own books on the subject. My purpose in writing the book was to propose a new way of thinking about recovery that would enhance the chance of recovery for those to whom it appealed. I also wanted to promote a deeper understanding of the value of the twelve-step program of Alcoholics Anonymous.

Campbell taught that there are eight stages to a heroic journey. They are: 1) the call to adventure; 2) refusal of the call (or wish to refuse); 3) acceptance of the call and receipt of magical gifts or otherwise divine assistance; 4) the adventure itself; 5) attainment of the quest; 6) the call to return home; 7) the refusal of the call to return (or wish to refuse); and 8) the return home with the boon or treasure attained for the benefit of the community. An important thing to understand is that the journey is really two journeys in one. There is the adventure itself, and there is the inward journey in which the hero looks within and discovers his true self. Campbell identifies this inward journey as spiritual in nature. He makes a remarkable statement of the purpose of the heroic journey. He says it is to redeem the world. He also says that compassion (see) is what makes us human. Without compassion we have nothing of value, and we develop compassion on our heroic journey. What helped me the most in my search was my developing compassion for my higher power.

My hope is that people who are in the process of engaging in a recovery effort will see themselves as heroes on a quest. I believe that the experience of attempting to follow the heroic path is a highly beneficial way of seeking a higher power. And of course, my hope is that those who seek a higher power will find a higher power. Nevertheless, I also have come to understand that it is the journey itself that is most important and what life is all about.

Wisdom from *The Power of Myth*

"The person who thinks he has found the ultimate truth is wrong. There is an often-quoted verse in Sanskrit, which appears in the Chinese *Tao-te Ching* as well: 'He who thinks he knows, doesn't know. He who knows that he doesn't know, knows." [28]

"The ultimate dragon is within you; it is your ego clamping you down." [29]

---

[28] Joseph Campbell with Bill Moyers, *The Power of Myth*, Anchor Books, 1991, 65.
[29] Ibid.,184.

Character assets needed in the search for a higher power

While the second step calls for a "coming to believe," the depth of this belief takes time to develop. At first it may be based on no more than seeing that the twelve-step approach is working for others. Newcomers who don't know what to make of the second step are typically told not to worry about "the God stuff." In recovery much emphasis is placed on character development. Character is often in short supply in the life of the active addict. A reading of the steps could leave a person bewildered, given that other than admitting to loss of control (step 1) and helping other alcoholics (step 12) there is nothing in the steps about drinking (or not drinking). The remainder of the steps have everything to do with character development. I maintain that as character develops people gain a meaningful sense of their higher power. Seeking a higher power is a process rather than an event, and it proceeds, importantly, in part from the development of positive character traits. I focus on five of these as indispensable to the successful search. They are honesty, forgiveness, gratitude, compassion, and lovingkindness.

Honesty

As we pass through our formative years, we acquire an astounding amount of information that we rely on as we adjust to the demands of the adult world. Inevitably, some of the information is incorrect, or we use correct information to reach incorrect conclusions. In either case, we develop ideas about ourselves and about the world that lead us to bad decisions or misperceptions. At the same time, we develop resistance to changing our minds when things are not working out as we hope, or as we think they ought to go. Let's think about two categories of things we learn about: we come to know about ourselves, and we learn about the rest of the world. As time goes on, each day, new data comes in that can either reinforce our ideas or suggest that a fact needs to be challenged. Our ego seeks to defend itself, and one of the dreaded dangers to the ego is being wrong. Thus, we resist being challenged about our opinions and beliefs. This tendency, this liability, represents an absolute obstacle to recovery from addiction and to spiritual growth. Even if we have a religious set of beliefs that seems to work for us, we must realize that as we mature our understanding of what we believe must deepen. People who are not open to this kind of learning have little possibility of a successful search for a higher power. So, the first rule of the search is to be *completely honest with ourselves.* The second rule is to have an open mind. The third is to be willing to follow the path to wherever it leads. The fourth rule is to not venture out by ourselves. Only we can do it, but we can't do it alone. Regarding powerlessness, think of the power that a wave may have over the ocean—none.

In addition to lying to ourselves, we also lie to others. Usually, this has become a habitual coping mechanism that we engage in almost unconsciously. Recovery demands that we let go of this type of dishonesty as well.

The Wisdom of others:

Alcoholics Anonymous

"We learned that we had to concede to our innermost selves that we were alcoholics. This is the first step in recovery. The delusion that we are like other people, or presently may be, has to be smashed."[30]

Twelve Steps and Twelve Traditions

"We perceive that only through utter defeat are we able to take our first steps towards liberation and strength. Our admissions of personal powerlessness finally turn out to be firm bedrock upon which happy and purposeful lives may be built."[31]

"The principle that we shall find no enduring strength until we first admit complete defeat is the main taproot from which our whole Society has sprung and flowered."[32]

---

[30] *Alcoholics Anonymous*, 30.
[31] *Twelve Steps and Twelve Traditions*, 21.
[32] Ibid., 22.

Michael Cowl Gordon

Forgiveness

Of the obstacles that can inhibit the process of seeking a higher power, none is greater than holding on to resentments. While this applies to all resentments, in the process of searching for a higher power it most particularly applies to resentments held against God, against people who have represented God to us, and against ourselves. We resent God because he has not been what we were told he would be. We were told God loves us, and we feel unloved. We were told God would protect us, and we feel unprotected. We were told God would prevent bad things from happening, and we find our world in a deplorable state. We were told God would heal the sick and loved ones have died or remained sick and disabled. We were told God is all-powerful and could do whatever God wants to do, and yet dreadful things happen every day. We were told God will answer our prayers, and we feel ignored.

We are told that whatever higher power it is that we are seeking will relieve us of our trouble, whether it is alcoholism, some other addiction, deep grief or sadness, or other issue from which we can't escape. If this is true it must be a different sort of higher power than we have been hearing about all our lives. In order to seek a higher power successfully, we need to leave our old ideas about God in the past. And to do so we need to forgive God for not being as represented, forgive others for misrepresenting God to us, and forgive ourselves for believing what proved to be untrue. This will be challenging, but the biggest step in the process is willingness to change. We are stepping into an abyss in which we are abandoning God A without knowing what God B will be like (or if there even is a God B). Understanding that it is necessary makes it easier to take this step, and it does say in the Big Book that if we seek a higher power we will succeed in our quest for a better life. And we are encouraged to believe in a higher power of our own choosing, so we can describe this higher power on our own terms. Willingness to take this step typically leads to a feeling of the old chains dropping away, and to the easing of the bonds to the prison of hating God, others, and ourselves.

In *The Divine Within* Aldous Huxley reflects on the Lord's Prayer. "As we forgive, we shall become progressively more capable of hallowing the name of God, of doing God's will and cooperating with God to make His kingdom come."[33] He identifies a direct cause and effect between being a forgiving person and becoming more connected to a higher power in our awareness. And there is another important point implied in his statement. By saying that we shall become progressively more capable, he suggests that it won't happen all at once. For most people it is indeed a gradual process, that of becoming a willing seeker of a higher power, let alone a finder of a higher power. Moreover, people will find themselves more successful in this forgiveness business on some days than others, or indeed, some moments more than others. So along with everything else, patience is called for.

The Wisdom of Others

Mishkan Hanefesh for Rosh Hashanah

In a prayer book for *Rosh Hashanah*, when Jewish people approach God as a community to ask for forgiveness, we find the following story. "Rabbi Israel Salanter once spent the night at a shoemaker's home. Late at night, he saw the man working by the light of a flickering candle. 'Look how late it is,' the rabbi said. 'Your candle is about to go out. Why are you still working?' The shoemaker replied, 'As long as the candle is burning, it is still possible to mend.' For weeks afterward, Rabbi Salanter was heard repeating the shoemaker's words to himself. 'As long as the candle is burning, it is still possible to mend.' As long as the candle burns—as long as the spark of life still shines—we can mend and heal, seek forgiveness and reconciliation, begin again."[34]

---

[33] Aldous Huxley, *The Divine Within*, Harper Perennial Modern Classics, 1992, 154.
[34] *Mishkan HaNefesh: Machzor for the Days of Awe, Rosh Hashanah*, Central Conference of American Rabbis, 2015, 81.

Michael Cowl Gordon

Alcoholics Anonymous

"Resentment is the number one offender. It destroys more alcoholics than anything else. From it stems all forms of spiritual disease, for we not only have been physically and mentally ill, we have been spiritually sick."[35]

Twelve Steps and Twelve Traditions

"This vital step (5th) was also the means by which we began to get the feeling that we could be forgiven, no matter what we had thought or done."[36]

Confucius

"To be wronged is nothing unless you continue to remember it."[37]

Ernest Kurtz and Katherine Ketcham

"...the opposite of 'resentment' is forgiveness."[38]

"Forgiveness inspires change."[39]

Quoting Lewis Hyde: "We forgive once we give up attachment to our wounds."[40]

Quoting Anne Lamott: "Forgiveness is giving up all hope of having had a better past."[41]

---

[35] *Alcoholics Anonymous*, 64.
[36] *Twelve Steps and Twelve Traditions*, 57-58.
[37] https://goodreads.com>quotes>15321.Confucius.
[38] Ernest Kurtz and Katherine Ketcham, *The Spirituality of Imperfection: Storytelling and the Search for Meaning*, Bantam Books, 1992, 215.
[39] Ernest Kurtz and Katherine Ketcham, *Experiencing Spirituality: Finding Meaning Through Storytelling*, Jeremy P. Tarcher/Penguin, 2014, 120.
[40] Ibid., 122.
[41] Ibid., 122.

Archbishop Desmond Tutu

"Forgiveness is the only way to heal ourselves and to be free from the past …. 'Without forgiveness, we remain tethered to the person who harmed us. We are bound to the chains of bitterness, tied together, trapped. Until we can forgive the person who harmed us, that person will hold the keys to our happiness, that person will be our jailor."[42]

---

[42] His Holiness, the Dalai Lama, Archbishop Desmond Tutu, with Douglas Abrams. *The Book of Joy: Lasting Happiness in a Changing World,* Avery, 2016, 234.

Gratitude

In seeking a higher power major potential obstacles include cynicism and negativity. The worst of these forms of negativity are self-pity and resentment. So, once again we are looking at resentment. Such attitudes are generally well-developed and deeply seated in the personality by the time a person reaches adulthood, especially since most people have reasonable grounds for such opinions. Too often as an aspect of this negativity is a bad attitude towards God, or if you prefer, a higher power.

It is worth pointing out that resentment and self-pity are two sides of the same coin. Any resentment list can be retitled as a self-pity list, and vice versa. The biggest challenge here is to become willing to reexamine treasured beliefs about why one's luck has been so bad, why the world is against one, why whatever one tries one always winds up at the same dead end. But first, one must work on being grateful. To challenge the negative beliefs directly may well result in more negativity.

Another potential roadblock can be a sense of entitlement. Many people are preoccupied with the thought that they deserve more or better in life than they have received. Such a sense of entitlement inevitably leads to feelings of resentment when the expectations are not met. Furthermore, a sense of entitlement creates conflict with other people who may want something for themselves as well. Issues of romance, money, employment, prestige, or other opportunities can lead to competition in which there is an apparent winner, and of course, a loser.

In my experience, the best way to overcome both resentment and self-pity is to focus on gratitude. It is not possible to be both grateful and resentful or self-pitying at the same time. At the beginning of this exercise all that is required is to try to identify something to be grateful for. Starting with such a burden of negativity, it may not be useful to concentrate on a search for a higher power at this stage. It may need to be a stepwise process. Focusing on the higher power itself is more helpful once we have released some of our anger and negativity. Anyone can find something to be grateful for if they are willing to keep it basic. Try feeling grateful for the air that you breathe—for food that you eat— for clothes that you wear, or for shelter. Some people may have only one or two of these basic necessities, but even that is a place to start. And most people can find something or someone to be grateful for beyond these necessities. Here it is worthwhile pointing out that a person can't try this once and expect transformation. It must become a daily practice, many times per day.

Opening oneself up to gratitude can be the beginning of a broader positive experience in one's life. Grateful thoughts will lead to a grateful heart and the beginning of a sense of peacefulness. The human spiritual dimension is touched, and as it is felt it will represent another source of gratitude. People who have previously been regarded as potential or actual enemies can begin to be seen in a neutral light, or even as friends, as people whom we wish to reach out to in a helpful or even loving way. As we find ourselves redefining ourselves and those about us in an environment of respect and love, gratitude will increase still more.

Having become grateful we will eventually start to think about just to what or to whom we owe this sea-change in our lives. Now the idea of a benevolent higher power arises, and as time goes on it makes more sense. As loving positive thoughts replace angry negative ones, the soil is prepared for a higher power experience.

The Wisdom of Others

Many spiritual people have expressed the value of gratitude on life's journey. Here are some of their thoughts. The first several of these come from the *Word for the Day* published by gratefulness.org.

Willie Nelson

"When I started counting my blessings, my whole life turned around."

Rumi

"Giving thanks for abundance is sweeter than the abundance itself."

"What is love? Gratitude. What is hidden in our chests? Laughter. What else? Compassion."

Melody Beattie

"Gratitude unlocks the fullness of life. It turns what we have into enough, and more."

Albert Nolan

"The grateful heart is a manifestation of one's true self. Nothing sidelines the ego more effectively than a grateful heart."

Ann Voskamp

"The art of deep seeing makes gratitude possible. And it is the art of gratitude that makes joy possible."

Simran Jeet Singh

"Gratitude is the practice that opens up hope."

Archbishop Desmond Tutu, His Holiness,
The Dalai Lama, and Douglas Abrams

They cite research findings of psychologist Sonja Lyubomirsky. "The three factors that seem to have the greatest influence on increasing our happiness are our ability to reframe our situation more positively, our ability to experience gratitude, and our choice to be kind and generous."[43]

They quote Brother David Steindl-Rast

"It is not happiness that makes people grateful. It is gratefulness that makes us happy."[44]

"Acceptance means not fighting reality. Gratitude means accepting reality."[45]

Anne Lamott

"Gratitude, not understanding, is the secret to joy and equanimity."[46]

Alan Morinis

Quoting Rabbi Shlomo Wolbe (1914-2005)

"Gratitude brings one to love, which is why this quality is so central. Love without gratitude has no ability to endure."[47]

Abraham Joshua Heschel

"It is gratefulness which makes the soul great." [48]

---

[43] *The Book of Joy*, 49.

[44] Ibid., 242.

[45] Ibid., 243

[46] Anne Lamott, *Plan B: Further Thoughts on Faith*, Riverhead Books, 2005, 295.

[47] *Every Day, Holy Day*, 188.

[48] Abraham Joshua Heschel, edited by Samuel Dresler, *I Asked for Wonder*, Crossroad, 1993, 22.

Rev. Charles F. Moon III

This quote challenges us to think more deeply, but it is worth the effort. He starts by mentioning spirituality as one of the fruits of our search for a higher power. Here he indicates that gratitude comes about because of the search itself. He identifies the need to be in control as a major obstacle in the search for a higher power, and circles back to Bill Wilson's realization that the alcoholic, without thinking about it or realizing it, tries to play God. Nobody will search for a higher power while seated on the throne. Chuck Moon was a Methodist Minister, a dear friend of mine, and I miss him.

"Spirituality itself is a gift; no one can acquire it or possess it, for it is a reality freely given and gratitude is the only possible response to this gift. In this response of gratitude, we begin to gain a vision of how truly gifted we really are. That vision, which comes only to those who in some way have given up trying to control, makes it possible to help in giving up other areas of control. We give up control because we realize we were never in control. It was an illusion based on our efforts to play God."[49]

---

[49] Rev. Charles F. Moon III, *Relevant Rambles: Musings of a Methodist Preacher in Recovery,* Powerful Potential & Purpose Publishing, 2021, 179.

Compassion

Compassion is the experience of acknowledging the pain or sadness of another with both the mind and the heart. As compassionate people we can relate to others at the point of their great sorrow. In so doing we experience the connectivity we have with the rest of the world, enabling us to reach the peak of our human potential. We cannot do this if we have not suffered ourselves. As we enlarge our own experience of the world, our sense of fear of others and of isolation diminishes. Such experiences can be of great help in the search for a higher power. First, as we allow ourselves to be more connected with others in an empathetic way, feeling more a part of the world, we are more able to accept the limits of our power, our capacity to control events, other people, and even ourselves. With this willingness to be accepting of life as it is, with this newfound wisdom as we reduce our sense of being our own higher power, we start to make room for a new higher power. This new higher power can become more real to us if we are open to the experience and demonstrate the willingness to be contemplative, to think, and to meditate on what is going on within and around us. Secondly, in the process we find ourselves caring about and even loving others, and more remarkably, ourselves. Love has the capacity to heal us from the inside out, and it is truly within ourselves that the higher power is most likely to be found.

This leads us to a third way that compassion can help us in our search for a higher power. Like everything else in this book, this won't work for everyone, but it is my strongest suggestion in the search. *Imagine for a moment that there is a loving Creator, who for the purpose of this example we will call God. Imagine that, as suggested by the poet James Weldon Johnson, God was lonely and decided to make a world. Imagine that God was pure loving energy but lacked an object to love. Imagine that out of this need God created the universe and set things in motion so that humans would make their appearance. Imagine that it is only through these humans that God can be acknowledged and loved in return. Now imagine that the humans defile the world, form themselves into little groups that hate and mistreat each other, and then blame God for everything that is wrong with the world. Now imagine how hurt God must feel by this state of affairs. This is a higher power that I can have compassion for. This is a higher power who has made no demands upon me, who doesn't need my worship or praise, who didn't create a devil who is setting traps for me so I will sin, who wants nothing more from me than to love this higher power in return for the higher power loving me. As I feel compassion for this higher power, my heart softens, and it opens up to the ocean of loving energy that I can now imagine pervading my existence. The God that was misrepresented to me as angry and vengeful fades from my consciousness. I can forgive those who made these misrepresentations to me, forgive God for allowing all the terrible things to happen to me and to others, and forgive myself for falling prey to such misunderstanding and for disrespecting and hating God. All this can begin with a decision to have compassion for God. This may not work for you, but it does work for me, every day that I do it.*

The Wisdom of Others

Joseph Campbell with Bill Moyers

"Compassion…. Is the healing principle that makes life possible."[50]

"I think of compassion as the fundamental religious experience and, unless that is there, you have nothing."[51]

William Alexander

"The final part of Step Eleven speaks of 'the power to carry it (God's will) out.' I believe that the persistence required to maintain my sobriety is resolutely joined to my practice of 'God's will.' If I am to stay sober, I must move from great thirst to great compassion. The power to carry out 'God's will' or the divine purpose—to a Buddhist, enlightenment for all beings—is found in *maitri-karuna*: love."[52]

---

[50] *The Power of Myth*, 112.

[51] Ibid., 212.

[52] *Ordinary Recovery: Mindfulness, Addiction, and the Path of Lifelong Sobriety*, 88-89.

MCG - Here is a deeply expressed understanding of how seeking our higher power leads us to love: "from great thirst to great compassion."

Abraham Joshua Heschel

".... when religion speaks only in the name of authority rather than the voice of compassion—its message becomes meaningless."[53]

Archbishop Desmond Tutu

"Ultimately our greatest joy is when we seek to do good for others. It's how we are made. I mean we are wired to be compassionate."[54]

---

[53] *God in Search of Man*, 3.
[54] *The Book of Joy*, 59.

Lovingkindness

Lovingkindness is the action that is prompted by compassion for others. It is not enough to care about others. We must reach out and help those in need when we are able to do so. In Buddhism (see), lovingkindness is so important that it is included as one of the four elements that comprise the idealized sublime state achieved through meditation and right conduct. The other three are compassion, sympathetic joy, and equanimity. The challenge here is to not only be good to people, but to love them unconditionally. I doubt that anyone can do this perfectly, but nevertheless it is important to make the effort. We are not just seeking a higher power. We are seeking happiness, love, validation, acceptance, and relief from our addictions and afflictions. Remember that we are embarking on this search for a higher power to gain relief from our alcoholism. It is more than just a good idea. If I need to be compassionate and be kind to all the people and creatures that I encounter in the universe, then I had better be willing to do so.

Rabbi Abraham Joshua Heschel and "Radical Amazement"

The over-riding thought expressed by Rabbi Heschel in his theology is that the first move is on the part of God— that man wouldn't even seek God if God did not seek man first. The day I came across his book, *God in Search of Man*, my entire spiritual search came into focus. The idea that God seeks man made perfect sense to me. I have since encountered many other great spiritual masters who believed the same thing, especially Meister Eckhart. The idea that God is concerned about man makes much more sense than the idea that God created the world with little or no regard for man. If we are more concerned with our world and life than God is, then we are better than God, an illogical presumption.

Rabbi Heschel was born in Poland in 1907, and he died in New York City in 1972. Both parents were raised in the Hasidic tradition of Judaism and were descended from the great leaders of the Hasidic movement. He received a classical education in Jewish studies, was ordained as a rabbi, and went to Berlin to study philosophy. He stayed in Germany to teach, but in 1938 was arrested by the Gestapo and deported to Poland. He was rescued the following year through the influence of Jewish friends and left for London six weeks before the German invasion of Poland. In 1940 he arrived in the United States. He taught at the Hebrew Union College in Cincinnati for 5 years and then spent the remainder of his life teaching at the Jewish Theological Seminary of America in New York City. He wrote many books, lectured all over the world, and was active in the American civil rights movement including marching with Dr. Martin Luther King in

Selma. Dr. King referred to Rabbi Heschel as "a truly great prophet."[55] He was active as well in ecumenism and played an important role representing American Jews at the Second Vatican Council.

Rabbi Heschel referred to his philosophy as "depth theology." By this he meant that thinking about God and the expression of ideas about God, which is what traditional theology deals with, must be preceded by a feeling experience that awakens the soul to the presence and concern of God. Such an experience may be triggered by suffering and also may be triggered by a sense of wonder. (see) Such an experience triggers a feeling, not just of wonder and awe, but of "radical amazement."[56] He says that it is curiosity that leads to philosophic thinking, but that it is wonder that leads to the understanding of God as sympathetic to human concern. It is fair to think of Rabbi Heschel as a mystic, as a person who recognizes that there is something beyond what we see in the world, something that is suggested by the world if only we are open to such awareness. And, when we truly contemplate the remarkable universe and all that exists within it, according to Heschel it seems that the existence of God is actually more plausible than that of the universe—the existence of God at times seems more likely than that which we see and know.

Again, the most significant idea of his is that man would never even think about God or seek God if God did not seek out man first. He sees man as needed by God in order to redeem the world, and in order to have a meaningful place in the world. Only man is capable of approaching God as a loving partner in the appreciation and repair of the world. He speaks of the "divine pathos," God's sadness, which can only be met by us with compassion for a God who suffers along with us. He says that if God was not saddened by our suffering, as we are moved by the suffering of others, then we would be better than God is, a theological impossibility. In all my reading, I have been touched the most deeply by these ideas. In the Suggested Reading appendix, I list several of his books which I

---

[55] https://kinginstitute.stanford.edu/heschel-abraham-joshua.

[56] Abraham Joshua Heschel, *Man Is Not Alone: A Philosophy of Religion*, Farrar, Straus, & Giroux, 1951, 11ff.

recommend, and it also might be helpful to read John C. Merkle's book wherein he explains these ideas.

The Wisdom of Abraham Joshua Heschel

From *God in Search of Man*

"Awareness of the divine begins in wonder." [57]

"All creative thinking comes out of an encounter with the unknown."[58]

From *Man Is Not Alone*

"What gives birth to religion is not intellectual curiosity but the fact and experience of our being asked. All that is left to us is a choice—to answer or to refuse to answer. Yet the more deeply we listen, the more we become stripped of the arrogance and callousness which alone would enable us to refuse."[59]
MCG – Ego deflation at depth.

"God is more plausible than our own selves."[60]

From *Man's Quest for God*

"Prayer may not save us, but prayer makes us worth saving. Of all the sacred acts, first comes prayer.... Religion is what man does with the presence of God. And the spirit of God is present whenever we are willing to accept it." [61]

---

[57] *God in Search of Man*, 46.

[58] Ibid., 114-115.

[59] *Man Is Not Alone*, 69.

[60] Ibid., 70.

[61] Abraham Joshua Heschel, *Man's Quest for God: Studies in Prayer and Symbolism*, Charles Scribner's Sons, 1954, xiv.

"Prayer is… no substitute for action. It is, rather, like a beam thrown from a flashlight into the darkness." [62]

"Prayer is not a thought that rambles alone in the world, but an event that starts in man and ends in God." [63]

"The thirst for companionship, which drives us so often into error and adventure, indicates the intense loneliness from which we suffer…It is such a sense of solitude which prompts the heart to seek the companionship of God…For man is incapable of being alone." [64]

"There is something which is far greater than my desire to pray, namely, God's desire that I pray. There is something which is far greater than my will to believe, namely, God's will that I believe." [65] MCG – This sounds like Thomas Merton.

---

[62] Ibid., 8.
[63] Ibid., 13.
[64] Ibid., 17.
[65] Ibid., 58.

Beauty as a gateway to a higher power

The appreciation of beautiful things is a major source of pleasure in life. We experience beauty in nature, music, art, poetry, and in the love and kindnesses we find in the world. Such an experience of beauty often opens us to considering the source of such beauty, and we thereby think about a creative process afoot in the world. We wonder about how such beauty could exist without a master artist being involved. It stretches our imagination as we consider the possibility of a creative intelligence or a spirit of the universe. Rabbi Heschel, about whom I wrote in the previous essay, places great emphasis on his belief that one of the primary ways that a higher power gets our attention is through the amazing beauty that we find in our lives.

Awe and Wonder

In our search for a higher power, a good starting place is the experience of wonder and awe. Most of the time we experience life without these qualities, especially if we are not looking to be amazed. But having become searchers, we open a door to higher possibilities. If we are receptive to life, paying attention to our experiences, we will inevitably be struck with the wonder of something. It could be something small, such as watching a wasp building a nest, or a bud forming on a camellia bush. Or it could be something vast, such as the sky on a cloudless night, a mountain range, or the ocean. It could be something powerful such as a thunderstorm or a volcano. It could be something beautiful, such as one's spouse or child, a sunset, a flower, or a painting or sculpture. Wonder and awe point beyond the object of beauty towards the divine. The wonder of such an experience triggers the feeling of awe. It is not simply the awareness that there is something in the world of immense intelligence and beauty. It is the deep feeling we experience not in the mind but in the heart that is associated with the wondrousness that we encounter. By opening ourselves to wonder and awe we initiate a journey that will without question transform our seeking into some kind of finding. It is important to abandon all preconceived notions of what the finding will be. All that is necessary is being open to where our experience will lead us. It is an individual journey to our own truth, not to somebody else's truth.

Rabbi Heschel in his book on the philosophy of Judaism, *God in Search of Man*, stresses that awareness of the transcendent presence in the universe begins with awe and wonder, that awe precedes faith. Awe is a response to the wonder experienced in the contemplation of the universe in all its aspects. With such an idea, wonder and awe are best understood as starting points in our search. Openness to an honest search is a prerequisite to success. The willingness to be uplifted, to see beyond the mundane, to be impacted by awe and wonder, is the key to unlocking the door to a higher awareness. The foundation idea of Heschel's theology is that wonder leads to *radical amazement*. So, in our search for a higher power, we need to be open to being blown away by life itself.

In the Hebrew Bible a virtue one is advised to seek to develop is *yirah* (Proverbs 9:10, "The fear of the Lord is the beginning of wisdom.").[66] However, *Yirah* can be translated both as fear and as awe. The difference between the two is immense. Fear, affecting my mind, causes me to withdraw from the fearsome force. Awe, affecting my heart, draws me towards it. In searching for a higher power, a power that is to help me do what I cannot do for myself, I hope to find a benevolent power, one that will support me, not frighten me.

According to Rabbi Heschel we would never even seek God if God did not invite us to seek God. He maintains that one of the mechanisms God employs is to fill us with wonder and awe, to amaze us with the immensity and beauty of the world, to let us know that what we experience alludes to something greater, more profound, beyond our capacity to fully imagine. Were it not for the invitation from God to come to the party as God's guest, we would never know about the party. Our job is to act on the invitation, to seek a relationship with this mysterious higher power. It is in this sense that even those who believe in the existence of God understand the limits of God's power. God can call us, but it is up to us to answer the call. Once engaged in this dialogue with the transcendent we go beyond belief into faith, a heart-awareness of the highest power. Going to church, by itself, can be a mechanical, habitual act. If not prepared to be amazed, we are not really seeking.

The Wisdom of Others

Abraham Joshua Heschel

"Much of the wisdom inherent in our consciousness is the root, rather than the fruit, of reason. There are more songs in our soul than the tongue is able to utter."[67]

---

[66] *NIV Holy Bible*, Zondervan, 2011, *Proverbs*, 343.
[67] *Man Is not Alone*, 17.

Michael Cowl Gordon

MCG – This is deep, expressed beautifully, and calls to mind the idea of the collective unconscious of Dr. Jung (see). It also agrees with Bill Wilson (see), who wrote in *Alcoholics Anonymous* that "Deep within every man, woman, and child is the idea of God."[68] I find it helpful and interesting that such great minds can independently arrive at such similar conclusions.

"What we encounter in our perception of the sublime, in our radical amazement, is a spiritual suggestiveness of reality, an allusiveness to transcendent meaning. The world in its grandeur is full of a spiritual radiance, for which we have neither name nor concept."[69]

'We sense His presence behind the splendor."[70]

Richard Rohr's Daily Meditation

"For Father Richard, contemplation... deepens our capacity to be amazed."[71]

MCG – Prayer and especially, meditation (see), can prepare the soil of our capacity to respond in our search into the mystery (see).

---

[68] *Alcoholics Anonymous*, 55.
[69] *Man Is not Alone*, 22.
[70] Ibid., 70.
[71] Richard Rohr's Daily Meditation. meditation@cac.org, *We Are What We See*, Monday, December 4, 2023.

Art

When I speak here of art, I am referring to the visual arts: painting, sculpture, graphic design, drawings, architectural designs, landscape designs, photography, all sorts of animation—anything that is created by humans that stimulates the visual system of the brain. The visual system, once stimulated, rapidly connects to other areas of the brain, including the unconscious, triggering physical reactions, emotions, and thoughts of every description. Art leads to at least two levels of experience that can help in the seeking of a higher power. One has to do with beauty, stimulating awe and wonder (see). When we look at something we believe to be beautiful it evokes within us a deep appreciation for the image and for the person who created the image. Secondly, an image that we view may help us to see beyond the image, to imagine what it may represent to the artist or to ourselves. Because I lack the ability to create images that look like what I see in my mind, I have great admiration for those who can do so. People who have artistic gifts are challenged to think about how they can use their gift to create images that others will appreciate and admire. They may even hope that their image may trigger a spiritual experience in the viewer, touching the viewer deeply.

Art that helps us to see beyond the image can touch us deeply in our souls. It can warm our hearts and trigger a sense of spirituality (see). Of course, this is the intention of religious art such as statues of the Buddha, or images of the crucifixion or other scenes from the life story of Christ. But other images can trigger our spiritual sensibilities without specific religious references, and it is these images that may help those seeking a higher power who prefer to not associate spirituality with religion. (Such people may eventually take a further step in their path, but this is irrelevant to where they are at this stage of seeking.) Any experience in which a seeker can be surprised by even a hint of a spiritual sensation can be encouraging and create a desire for more progress in this domain. Such experiences also connect us in a feeling way to our unconscious minds as archetypal memories are triggered, memories that are present in the collective unconscious that connects us all (see – Carl Jung). We may realize that we can know much more than we thought we did, that our awareness of our universe has been repressed, and is less than it could or should be. Thus, art is a medium that has the potential to connect us to a powerful resource within ourselves. As such, it may serve as one of the many pathways in the process of our seeking a higher power.

Music

I don't know that I have ever met a person who does not enjoy music. (Even totally deaf people can feel vibrations and tempo and experience pleasure.) True, there are different tastes in music, but in some way, it seems to have a universal attraction for people. And yet, it is a challenge to put into words just how music exerts its effect on us. Music gets us out of the realm of the rational and into a world beyond verbal expression. It stimulates multiple areas of the brain as it accomplishes its magic. It stimulates our feeling world, potentially at every level. Music can make us feel happy, joyful, sad, or excited. It can stimulate our sense of connection with others. Music can make us want to jump up and move around, to dance, to march, to tap out the rhythm with our feet or clap our hands. Certain songs can make us nostalgic as pleasant memories are stirred. Significantly, music can touch us in our spiritual core, our soul (see). Many people are gifted with the ability to play an instrument, sing, or compose songs or other kinds of music. For such people this creative outlet can open a channel to a connection with a higher power. Even for those lacking musical ability, listening to music can form a spiritual bond or pathway to higher power awareness.

Music, or what can easily be construed as music, exists in the natural world. This afternoon my wife and I took a walk in a nearby park and were treated to a variety of bird calls. We were entertained by a pair of barred owls calling to each other, probably asserting their territorial limits. Several other birds were calling as well. Tonight, when we sit on our porch, we will hear frogs and insects. Nature's songs are often related to mating behavior, just as humans sing and listen to love songs. Music often gets people "in the mood" as well.

Music or indeed any sound is generated by vibrations. People have a highly sophisticated auditory mechanism that is designed to detect vibrations and transmit them to the brain. The phenomenon of vibration in our world goes far beyond sounds that can be heard. Everything vibrates in some way. One of Einstein's most important early papers was on the cause of Brownian motion, the random motion of particles suspended in a medium. In fact, in the study of particle physics, which quite frankly is way beyond my comprehension, it seems that everything vibrates. In music, an important and powerful component is drumming. Drumming is also an important element of some religious ceremonies, the pulse of the drum being felt deeply in the participants body and soul, seemingly throbbing like a heartbeat.

Interestingly, one element of life that never intrudes into an AA meeting is music. Having said that, let me caution you never to take never as an absolute. I once was at an Al-Anon convention when a speaker burst into song. And now that zoom is a thing, people are experimenting with different kinds of meetings, including playing a song and then having a discussion.

If you think about it, if our universe started with a Big Bang, it must have made quite a noise. In fact, I believe physicists continue to find what they believe to be traces of that noise. A corollary to this statement is that there must have been total silence prior to the Big Bang.

The Wisdom of Others

Joseph Epes Brown quoting Black Elk

"The drum is often the only instrument used in our sacred rites.... It is especially sacred and important to us.... Because the round form of the drum represents the whole universe, and its strong steady beat is the pulse, the heart, throbbing at the center of the universe. It is as the voice of *Wakan-Tanka*, and this sound stirs us and helps us to understand the mystery and power of all things."[72]

---

[72] Joseph Epes Brown, *The Sacred Pipe: Black Elk's Account of the Seven Rites if the Oglala Sioux,* University of Oklahoma Press, 1953, 1989, 69.

Rabbi Nachman of Breslov (1772-1810)

"A person should get in the habit of singing, for a holy melody is a great and wondrous thing. It can awaken the heart from sleep and bring it back to the divine Source of all."[73]

Rumi

"There are many ways to the Divine; I have chosen music, dance, and laughter." [74]

---

[73] *Mishkan Hanefesh: Machzor for the Days of Awe – Yom Kippur,* Central Conference of American Rabbis, 2015, 171.
[74] https://www.azquotes.com/quote/1351657.

Poetry

Words can be wondrous things, at times conveying a sublime sense of beauty. Poetry is a word art-form that can for some people open the gates to a spiritual sensibility and experience. Not only can poets express themselves in a unique way, but they also perceive beauty and relationships where others may not. Any feeling can stimulate a person to write a poem and can invite the reader of a poem to relate to the expressed feeling. Of course, many people set their poems to music, and some of these songs continue to stir feelings in millions of people. Thus, poetry (and music) can be of great benefit in opening a channel to a higher power. But reading poetry can sometimes be demanding, because the poet's meaning may be obscure at first glance. We need to take the time and have the patience to fully appreciate the experience. Frequently poets use metaphor and paradox to jar us out of our concrete way of everyday thinking.

Here is a fragment of a poem from *The Prophet* by Khalil Gibran which I include here as an example of how poetry can stimulate us to think more deeply and be moved. It is striking for its use of imagery and paradox.

> *"For what is it to die but to stand naked in the wind and to melt into the sun?*
> *And what is it to cease breathing, but to free the breath from its restless tides, that it may rise and expand and seek God unencumbered?*
> *Only when you drink from the river of silence shall you indeed sing.*
> *And when you have reached the mountain top, then you shall begin to climb.*
> *And when the earth shall claim your limbs, then shall you truly dance."*

Many if not all people who experience contact with the Spirit in their heart, subsequently lose the connection. This can be a source of great consternation and confusion, although as time goes on, we learn how to feed our relationship with our higher power by attending twelve-step meetings, working the steps, and whatever other means that speak to us. The great poet and priest, St. John of the Cross called this loss of connection with a higher power The Dark Night of the Soul and he wrote a stunning poem about his experience. Here are the first few lines, quoted in and commented about in their book, *O Blessed Night,* by Francis Nemeck and Marie Coombs.

"The poem begins abruptly with the anxious cry of the soul in search of its Beloved:

> *'Where have you hidden yourself,*
> *O my Beloved, having left me in anguish?*
> *You fled like the deer,*
> *Having wounded me.*
> *I went forth searching frantically for you,*
> *And you were gone.'*

"That initial stanza sets the tone for all that follows. When God opens our hearts more deeply to Himself, we experience a painful wound of love. This wound becomes manifest in the agonizing realization that the Beloved has vanished without warning. Thus, we experience ourselves drowning in an ever more obscure sea of confusion. We set out anxiously searching."[75]

MCG – This underscores that the seeking of a higher power is another aspect of living one day at a time—and that some days we may find a higher power and other days we may not.

---

[75] Francis Kelley Nemeck, OMI, and Marie Theresa Coombs, Hermit, *O Blessed Night: Recovering from Addiction, Codependency, and Attachment Based on the Insights of St. John of the Cross and Pierre Teilhard de Chardin,* Alba House, Society of Saint Paul, 1991, 48.

Carl Jung – Psychology and Spirituality

Carl Jung was born in Switzerland in 1875 and died there in 1961. He came from a long line of ministers. As a child, Jung spent much time alone and entertained himself with his remarkable imagination. Jung's father, a minister who lost his faith in middle age, and Jung were distant from each other. Jung's relationship with his father had a profound influence on his own psychological development. His early success in psychological research gave him an international reputation, and led to him collaborating with the Austrian psychiatrist, Sigmund Freud starting in 1907. However, by 1912 their theoretical differences led to a split, and Jung proceeded to develop his ideas independently. As part of his exploration into the unconscious he engaged in a practice he called active imagination, and at times seemed to verge into madness. Two aspects of his relationship with Freud deserve note. One is that Freud had a habit of cutting colleagues off if they disagreed with his theories and developed their own theories. There can be no question that for a time Freud was a father figure to Jung, and that his loss of this relationship was devastating, especially given that he and his own father could never come to understand each other. The other aspect has to do with their basic theories. While they both relied heavily on the concept of the unconscious mind, Freud saw mental illness as the result of sexual repression. He had little appreciation for the spiritual dimension of man as he himself was an atheist. Jung on the other hand had a strong belief in God and recognized the significance and importance of the spiritual realm of life.

Jung's psychological research led him to conclude that mankind is connected by a commonly held "collective unconscious." He believed that certain ideas, patterns, and images, which he called "archetypes," are carried within the unconscious of us all, and that we are profoundly affected by these contents. He also developed ideas about what he termed complexes and coined the terms "introvert" and "extrovert" to describe basic personality types. He developed a theory of personality structure including both conscious and unconscious elements. The deepest level of the personality, the spiritual core, he termed the "self." Here the individual experiences union with the higher power, the God of his understanding. His goal in therapy with his patients was to help them to unify the components of the personality so that they could get the maximum satisfaction out of life. This was a spiritual as well as psychological experience that he called "individuation."

Dr. Jung played a significant role in the genesis of Alcoholics Anonymous that he was unaware of until not long before his death when he received a letter from Bill Wilson, a co-founder of AA. Jung had treated an alcoholic patient (Roland H.) who had not responded to his therapeutic approach and had returned to drinking. Returning to Jung, Roland asked for additional treatment, but Jung told him he had nothing else to offer him, and he suggested that he seek a spiritual or religious solution for his drinking problem. Roland returned to the US and affiliated himself with the Oxford movement with good success. An aspect of the Oxford Group program was the expectation of helping others. Roland learned of an alcoholic who was in trouble (Ebby T.), and he and two others got him out of jail and brought him to New York City where they exposed him to the Oxford Movement and worked with him in this context. After a couple of months, they told him it was time for him to reach out to someone and carry the message. Ebby called on his old friend Bill Wilson, and the ultimate result of this visit was Bill quit drinking, had a spiritual experience of his own, and set his purpose in life to carry his message of the spiritual solution of the problem of alcoholism to the world. In his letter to Dr. Jung, Bill explained this sequence of events and thanked him for having had the humility to admit that he couldn't help Roland with further treatment. Dr.

Jung responded with a letter in which he explained his view of the spiritual dimension in which alcoholism afflicts its victims.

How can the ideas of Dr. Jung help us seek a higher power? First, I suggest that a seeker give his ideas serious consideration. Jung was a brilliant man who spent his life searching for answers to understanding humanity, the universe, and the spiritual dimension of existence. Next, try to find something here that makes sense to you, that you might be able to use in your own search for a higher power. Also, you can embark on your own study of Jung through reading some of the suggested references in the back of this book. There are also on-line groups devoted to the study of Jung. I include below a few quotes of Jung, and of others who have studied or who share his thoughts. However, it is only fair to caution you that the study of Jung is challenging.

The Wisdom of Others

Chuck C.

MCG - Here Chuck is commenting about the correspondence between Bill Wilson and Dr. Jung.

"And Dr. Jung wrote back, and he told Bill, in essence, that he had always known that the alcoholic's problem was his search for unity.... his attempt to find unity with the life around him and with the God that made him. And when he found that bottle, it seemed to be the missing ingredient.... He had found chemical unity, and it did a pretty good job for him until it became the problem that only a spiritual answer could solve." [76]

Eric Ackroyd

"For Freud, religion was a neurosis; for Jung, religion was therapeutic— it was the ultimate cure for the troubled human psyche. The quest for one's

---

[76] Chuck C., *A New Pair of Glasses,* New-Look Publishing Company, 1984, 105.

own authentic self and the quest for God are, for Jung, one and the same quest." [77]

MCG - Thus, the higher power may be sought through a search for oneself on the heroic journey of life.

---

[77] Eric Ackroyd, *A Dictionary of Dream Symbols*, Blandford, 1993, 35.

Spirituality – A pathway to a higher power

Spirituality is a dimension of existence. Nevertheless, it has no form, that is, it is not composed of matter, as far as we can tell. The word is derived from the Latin, *spiritus*, which means "breath". As such, it can be related to the soul, the aspect of a person that exists beyond what we can observe or measure. It is sensed rather than observed, and not by the sense organs. We do not see, hear, touch, taste, or smell spirituality directly. We intuit the realm of spirituality in those moments when we think, "There must be more." A sense of spirituality is often triggered by wonder and awe (see) and forms the basis, in part, for the development of religion (see). The biggest difference between spirituality and religion is that religions develop specific beliefs about the realm of the spirit, whereas with spirituality we are not confined to concepts or dogma.

Many people in AA are fond of saying that they are spiritual but not religious. By this they simply mean that they believe there is something wondrous beyond what can be seen, but that they can't say exactly what, and really don't want to try to limit it with words. They are content to have the awareness that it exists. When people say, "I believe in something, but I don't know what it is," they are responding to a sensation within themselves unrelated to the five senses, a something that religion, in a way, talks about, but ruins for some people as much as it clarifies for others. Duane R. Bidwell writes about people who he refers to as SBNRs (Spiritual But Not Religious). "SBNRs reject religious exclusivism, dogmatism, judgment, and the concept of sin; advocate internal spiritual authority; make pragmatic and therapeutic use of spiritual practices to achieve liberation; and see nature as a source or mediator of spirituality. They have a strong commitment to a universal truth that underlies all religions, and they see internal happiness and peace as the ultimate goals of spirituality."[78] If I could have said this better, I would have done so. But by taking on this position, we must avoid the trap of laziness—of telling ourselves that just because a higher power will resist a certainty of identity that we needn't bother to engage in the search. But search we must, for it

---

[78] Duane R. Bidwell, *When One Religion Isn't Enough: The Lives of Spiritually Fluid People*, Beacon Press, 2018, 41-42.

seems that the search itself is what we must experience to bring spirituality into our lives. If we cultivate the qualities of love, compassion, awe, wonder, justice and humility we will find enough of what we are seeking, and we realize that what we seek has always been within us. Once people realize this, they also realize that they are not God, and they can stop trying to control by playing God. Ernest Kurtz realized this to be such a basic precept of Alcoholics Anonymous that he called his pioneering history of Alcoholics Anonymous *Not-God.*[79]

The Wisdom of Others

Rabbi Rami Shapiro

"What I mean by spiritual growth is this: an ever-deepening capacity to embrace life with justice, compassion, curiosity, awe, wonder, serenity, and humility."[80]

MCG – I like to equate the journey of spiritual growth with the journey of seeking a higher power. That is, the emphasis is on the journey itself. If we cultivate the above qualities as we travel through life, we will see that it is the same journey, and our seeking will, to some extent, transition into finding.

Came to Believe – AA World Services

"Our concepts of a Higher Power and God—as we understand Him— offer everyone a nearly unlimited choice of spiritual belief and action."[81]

---

[79] Ernest Kurtz, *Not-God: A History of Alcoholics Anonymous*, Hazelden, 1979.
[80] Rami Shapiro, *Recovery, the Sacred Art: The Twelve Steps as Spiritual Practice*, SkyLight Paths Publishing, 2009, xiii.
[81] *Came to Believe: The Spiritual Adventure of AA as Experienced by Individual Members*, Alcoholics Anonymous World Services, Inc., 1973, 77. From a Grapevine article by Bill Wilson, April 1961.

"We are not healed by love alone, but by our response to love. Our understanding of God grows through our willing response to Him."[82]

Alcoholics Anonymous

"We finally saw that faith in some kind of God was part of our make-up, just as much as the feeling we have for a friend. Sometimes we had to search fearlessly, but He was there. He was as much a fact as we were. We found the Great Reality deep down within us. In the last analysis it is only there that He may be found. It was so with us."[83]

Mel Ash

MCG - He talks about what Bill Wilson got from William James' *The Varieties of Religious Experience:*

"Complete deflation at depth, meaning deflation of the overinflated ego and sense of one's uniqueness, was what was required to ready the recipient for the experience. Bill understood immediately that this is what had happened to him. He had surrendered enough of his old ideas and beliefs about life to become willing to be filled with something bigger and more universal."[84]

"When we are free to define the power greater than ourselves, we invariably choose one that is essentially an extension of our deepest yearnings and noblest hopes. It is a Higher Power that we feel a part of and not apart from. A natural relationship is resumed between us and our source of existence, whatever we choose to call it." [85]

MCG - Here I should say – give the advice that – people really should choose a higher power that they find likeable.

---

[82] Ibid., 98.
[83] *Alcoholics Anonymous*, 55.
[84] Mel Ash, *The Zen of Recovery*, Jeremy P. Tarcher/Putnam, 1993, 54.
[85] Ibid., 68.

Richard Rohr's Daily Meditations

"As James Finley says, 'The greatest teacher of God's presence in our life is our life.'" [86]

Heard at an AA meeting

"We are not human beings having a spiritual experience; we are spiritual beings having a human experience."

---

[86] *Richard Rohr's Daily Meditations*, meditations@cac.org., *Facing Reality to Awaken Ourselves*, Friday, March 15, 2024.

Love

Love is another important means of seeking a higher power. I am talking more about love as an action rather than love as a thought or a feeling. This is a practical matter. We have already examined and hopefully agreed on the idea that God is not fully comprehensible. This being the case, "figuring it out" is going to get us nowhere. We need to "act as if" higher power is real and approach this entity in another way. My proposal here is that we use love as an approach to a higher power. I suggest that the seeker shift entirely from head to heart. Stop thinking about who, what, or where the higher power might be. Instead, simply engage in a loving action towards your higher power, whatever this might mean to you at this time. This may feel bizarre and make no sense. It doesn't matter. Do it anyway. Sit quietly, become centered in your heart, and engage in loving feelings. This may be problematic for people who have lost touch with their loving feelings and have become mired in bitterness and self-hate. Some seekers may be starting on empty. Paradoxically, this may be an ideal place from which to begin the search— utter demoralization and feeling absolutely lost and abandoned. From just such a place can one decide that if this is where their best efforts have brought them, they might as well try something else, however ridiculous a suggestion may appear to be. First, it may help to engage in a loving action towards a more concrete entity, such as a person, if the action of feeling love for a higher power seems impossible to wrap your head around. Greet a stranger without expectation of getting anything in return. Pay for someone's coffee. Pick up a few pieces of trash along the road or in a parking lot. Start to take actions that help you feel connected to the universe. By so doing the world will feel less like a hostile place, and you may start to feel as though you belong inside of it.

As you engage in these actions be open to having positive feelings for other people. If you have started to attend a recovery fellowship, try to have positive feelings for the other people there. Others may approach you in such a way that it appears that they are glad to see you, to have you as part of the group. At this point you may start to think about what you are experiencing. As you think, you may see that you are like other people, and that your self-hate is a distorted perception based on the horrible addictive abyss that has pulled you into its grasp. Now try to engage in loving feelings again. Try to feel love for the other people in the fellowship. If you are on a bus or in a store, feel love for the people with whom you are sharing space. Think if there is one person in your life for whom you still have loving feelings, even if the feelings may seem to be unreciprocated. Go ahead and direct some love-energy towards that person. Do these things every day, many times each day. Once you have engaged your heart in this way, and have repeated the activity many times, you may be ready to widen the scope to include yourself. Try to have loving feelings for yourself. This is not a thinking exercise— stay with the heart (see). If it isn't working, stop, and try again another time. This may also be a time to try to direct heart-energy—loving feelings—again to a higher power. Don't spend hours at this. Just try it and see if it feels good, or at least if it doesn't feel bad. If you are not ready, wait a few days, or longer, but at some point, if you are opening your heart to care about others, and letting others care about you, then you will make progress on your search for a higher power by loving that which you cannot see, hear, touch, or understand. This might sound crazy, but as we have often heard, "don't knock it if you haven't tried it." People who sincerely commit to this exercise will experience positive results.

The Wisdom of Others

Archibald MacLeish

"Man depends on God for all things; God depends on man for one. Without man, God does not exist as God, only as creator, and love is the one thing no one, not even God Himself, can command. It is a free gift, or it is nothing. And it is most itself, most free, when it is offered in spite of suffering, of injustice, and of death."[87]

---

[87] https://www.azquotes.com/author/9220-Archibald_MacLeish.

The Bible - 1 John: 4:7-8

"Dear friends, let us love one another, for love comes from God. Everyone who loves has been born of God and knows God. Whoever does not love does not know God, because God is love."[88]

Erich Fromm

"...the main condition for the achievement of love is the overcoming of one's narcissism."[89]

"...while one is consciously afraid of not being loved, the real, though usually unconscious fear is that of loving."[90]

Aldous Huxley

Quotes Meister Eckhart – "Some people want to see God with their eyes as they see a cow, and to love Him as they love their cow—for the milk and cheese and the profit it brings them.... I tell you the truth, any object you have in your mind, however good, will be a barrier between you and the inmost Truth."[91]

---

[88] *NIV Holy Bible*, 656.

[89] Erich Fromm, *The Art of Loving*, Harper & Brothers Publishers, 1956, 118.

[90] Ibid.,127.

[91] Aldous Huxley, *The Perennial Philosophy*, Harper Perennial Modern Classics, 1945, 2009, 84.

Soul

Searching for a higher power will certainly have its challenges. In a way, it may be the most difficult journey we ever embark upon. We have spoken of recovery as a heroic journey (see), one into which we are forced because we find ourselves in the grip of an addiction that we realize is impossible to survive. Yet, we are promised success in this heroic endeavor if we accept the challenge and the gifts that are offered. We are told that we alone can do it, but that we can't do it alone. We are promised that recovery is available to all those who seek a higher power, and we are then given the freedom to search for a higher power of our choice. Possibly, choice is not really involved. Rather, we give it our best effort, and the higher power reveals itself to us in a way in which we can understand it—or if not understand it, at least accept whatever it seems to be without further questioning or judgment. We make peace with the higher power of either our understanding or our not understanding.

Where does soul enter the picture? Soul is the term we use to indicate the spiritual dimension of ourselves. It may not be accidental that in its depth the idea of soul is no more comprehensible than the idea of a higher power. This coincidence of ineffability suggests that the concepts are related—that soul and higher power have elements in common. As we seek our soul, we discover ourselves and our relationship with our creator.

One route to the understanding of soul, and therefore, of comprehending higher power, is to see what soul leaves in its wake. We experience awe and wonder when we look at the stars, the ocean, the development of an embryo. These are indicative of a power much beyond ourselves. Likewise, we witness the compassion expressed by ourselves and others—sacrifices made for our children, our communities, our families and friends, and by some of us, the capacity to love our enemies. The expression of compassion expresses a kind and degree of love that goes beyond the basic human survival needs of air, food, shelter, water, and reproduction. May there not be within each person a spirit as the source of compassion? Considering that such may be true is an important and useful awareness that facilitates the search for a higher power.

Therefore, I suggest that we include a search for our own soul as part of the search for a higher power. And it is important to realize that it is more the searching than the finding that matters. True, many will discover their own souls, and many will connect with a higher power. But it is in the search, in the journey that is the true finding. There is something dynamic about searching that it could stop when it results in a discovery. Discoveries can be made along the way, but if we stop searching, if we stop moving along a spiritual path, we will inevitably regress. There is no standing still in the search. This is why we are advised to be involved in the search daily, through the means of self-awareness, self-examination, meditation, prayer, and helping others (AA Steps 10, 11, and 12).

All the great teachers have said that the search for the soul must be preceded by suffering, and that you can't think your way into the search. On the other hand, we all can ignore the lessons we are being taught and learn nothing of our souls or of our higher power from our experience.

So, how do we find our soul? I suspect that it is findable in a way that will feel right, but that the important action is in the seeking. And I propose that the interior search for one's soul is a key to the search for a higher power. Meditation (see) will be useful in this regard. Thomas Merton and others write about solitude. Contemplation of a higher power can lead to contemplation of soul, and vice versa. If the soul is part of us, then we can think of it as having life. Life requires nourishment. What food does the soul require? I would suggest that the soul feeds on love, compassion, kindness, and all the selfless qualities that we can develop in ourselves while searching for our higher power. And again, from Thomas Merton and many others comes the idea that ultimate unity is found where we recognize that the spirit of the universe is found within each of us, equally, inseparably, and eternally. In my search I have found that this is a useful concept to contemplate, and I suggest that you think about it as you search for your own soul and your higher power.

The Wisdom of Others

Abraham Joshua Heschel

"Man is man because something divine is at stake in his existence. He is not an innocent bystander in the cosmic drama. There is in us more kinship with the divine than we are able to believe. The souls of man are candles of the Lord, lit on the cosmic way….and every soul is indispensable to Him. Man is needed, he is a need of God."[92]

Thomas Merton

"In order to find our own souls, we have to enter into our own solitude and learn to live with ourselves."[93]

"Man's greatest dignity, his most essential and peculiar power, the most intimate secret of his humanity is his capacity to love. This power in the depths of man's soul stamps him in the image and likeness of God."[94]

MCG - Here Father Merton sounds like Rabbi Heschel.

Matthew Fox

"Eckhart… teaches that the human soul is, like God, unknowable, unnamable, and ineffable, and he repeats the point on numerous occasions. He says, 'God, who is without a name—He has no name—is ineffable, and the soul in its ground is also ineffable, as He is ineffable.'"[95]

MCG – Thus, if there is such a thing as a soul, according to Eckhart it follows that there is also God, or if you prefer, a spirit of the universe.

---

[92] *I Asked for Wonder,* 54.
[93] Thomas Merton, *Disputed Questions,* Harcourt Brace Jovanovich,1985, xi.
[94] Ibid., 98.
[95] Matthew Fox, *Meister Eckhart: A Mystic-Warrior for Our Times,* Reprinted with permission by New World Library, www.newworldlibrary.com, 2014, 218-219.

Quotes Eckhart: "All human science can never fathom what the soul is in its ground.... What the soul is in its ground, no one knows. What one can know about it must be supernatural; it must be from grace. The soul is where God works compassion."[96]

MCG – Below is a meditation suggestion that may help you in your search. I love the image of waves in the ocean.

Sam Torode

"Cultivate your connection to spirit. Meditate on the unfathomable depths of your soul, and its union with the Source. Your soul is part of the universal soul, which is serene, whole, and perfect. It is an endless ocean of light, upon which our souls arise as waves."[97]

Frederic Gros

"Once you no longer expect anything from the world on those aimless and peaceful walks, that is when the world delivers itself to you."[98]

MCG – Here is the paradox of finding by letting go.

Richard Rohr

"I think of soul as anything's ultimate meaning which is held within. Soul is the blueprint inside of every created thing telling it what it is and what it can become. (MCG – Fascinating thought). When we meet anything at that level, we will respect, protect, and love it.[99]

---

[96] Ibid., 122.

[97] Sam Torode, *Living from the Soul: The 7 Spiritual Principles of Ralph Waldo Emerson*, www. samtorode.com, 2020, 51.

[98] Frederic Gros, *A Philosophy of Walking*, Verso, 2014, 2023, 52.

[99] Richard Rohr's Daily Meditation, meditations@cac.org, *The Soul of Nature*, Sunday March 3, 2024.

Heart

In their search for a higher power people typically set out by thinking, using the mind, the brain. While I believe it is safe to say that the human brain is the most complex and remarkable structure in the known universe, and while we can probably agree that the mind resides within the brain, it seems to be the case that not all problems can be solved by thinking. Indeed, the search for a higher power is likely to demand a feeling component as well as a thinking component. Thus, we need to consider where to seek a place within ourselves to direct the search, and the most likely candidate is the heart. The first thing all human beings hear in the womb is their mother's heartbeat. We tend to associate "heart-feeling" with warmth (warm-hearted), gentleness (soft-hearted), kindness (kind-hearted), and a welcoming spirit (open-hearted). Such feelings and tendencies, in the search for a higher power, act to suppress that great enemy of finding a higher power, the ungrateful ego. The practice of heart-awareness makes us cognizant of ourselves on a different plane, more open to the spiritual. A. W. Tozer refers to "spiritual receptivity" as an essential ingredient in the search for a higher power.[100] And it is within the realm of the spirit that the search for a higher power may well be pursued. Even for those for whom the idea of God never makes sense, but for whom the power of the group, or the vastness of the universe is the higher power that is found, there is a definite sense of spirituality that can be experienced in the heart. One method of seeking a higher power is to practice heart-awareness. Try to experience heart energy while meditating, instead of trying to think or to understand. It is not even necessary to do this in formal meditation practice.

---

[100] A.W. Tozer, *The Knowledge of the Holy, The Pursuit of God, God's Pursuit of Man, Three Spiritual Classics in One Volume,* Moody Publishers, 1948, 1950, 1961, 275.

The Wisdom of Others

Anne Lamott

Quoting her pastor, Veronica: "We don't transform ourselves, she said, but when we finally hear, the Spirit has access to our hearts, and that is what changes us."[101]

Matthew Fox

"He (Eckhart) connects the psyche and cosmos, heart and the heavens, when he says: 'Where should we begin? With the heart...Begin with the heart, which is the noblest part of the body. It lies in the center of the body from which point it bestows life on the whole body. For the spring of life arises in the heart and has an effect like heaven.'"[102]

MCG – Here and elsewhere we find a direct connection between heart and soul.

---

[101] *Plan B: Further Thoughts on Faith*, 225.
[102] *Meister Eckhart: A Mystic-Warrior for Our Times*, 215.

Connection

Man is essentially a social being. While "alone time" is something everyone seems to need, a greater need is companionship, a sense of belonging or connection to another person or group of people. People who have reached a "bottom" in their lives are typically at a point of great isolation from others. They have hidden or tried to hide from others their state of demoralization and sense of hopelessness. Now, in seeking a new solution to their problem, they are told that one reason they are in this condition is they tried to solve the problem by themselves. They need a new source of a remedy, what is being referred to as a higher power. Many if not most such people do not have a concept of a higher power that they can relate to in such a way that they can see how this will be of any help. For such people often the answer can be a recovery group. Walking into an AA group, for example, or zooming into one, can be a first of a kind experience where the people who claim to be alcoholic give every appearance of being happy, sober, and hopeful, while at the same time speaking freely about the horrors of their past lives of a few weeks, months, or years ago. Our newcomer may well hear the "God word" mentioned or see it plastered on the walls but doesn't need to let it be a turn-off if there is no comprehension of or belief in God at the time. Indeed, there may well be some animosity borne towards God for reasons related to personal tragedies of the past along with the belief that God is all powerful. How could a God who has permitted such tragedy now act with such grace as to elevate his life to a state of happiness, peacefulness, and enjoyment? Encouraged to not worry about the "God part of the program," he is advised to just not drink today, and to become part of the group. It is connection to the group that is the power greater than himself at this stage.

Another aspect of connection is the feeling of being connected to the universe. Indeed, the concept of unity is the bedrock of many of the great thinkers' ideas about the world. I include in this group Schrodinger, Jung, Campbell, the Buddha, and Einstein. In one way or another they talk of the importance of understanding that there is an energy force that pervades the entire universe, even into the being of everyone.

Of course, the idea of people working together is well understood in achieving success in any organization— in sports, at work, in politics, in business, at school, church, community service organizations, special interest clubs, and in family life. Even so, connection involves risk, the need to trust others or to trust a higher power. As such, it is not a choice made easily and indeed may never be made. But those who have risked it will attest that the risk has been more than worthwhile.

The Wisdom of Others

William Sloane Coffin

"We can build a community out of seekers of truth, but not out of possessors of truth."[103]

Fritjof Capra

"Although the various schools of Eastern mysticism differ in many details, they all emphasize the basic unity of the universe which is the central feature of their teachings. The highest aim for their followers— whether they are Buddhists, Hindus, or Taoists—is to become aware of the unity and mutual interrelation of all things, to transcend the notion of an isolated individual self and to identify themselves with the ultimate reality."[104]

Rev. Martin Luther King

"We are caught in an inescapable network of mutuality, tied in a single garment of destiny. Whatever affects one directly, affects all indirectly."[105]

---

[103] *Who Needs God?*, 194.
[104] Fritjof Capra, *The Tao of Physics: An Exploration of the Parallels between Modern Physics and Eastern Mysticism*, Shambala, 2010, 24.
[105] Martin Luther King, *Why We Can't Wait*, New York: New American Library, Harper & Row, 1964.

Mel Ash

"Zen… shows us how all our other diseases and discontents flow from our fundamental denial of unity with each other and the universe."[106]

Neil MacGregor

"One of the central facts of human existence is that every known society shares a set of beliefs and assumptions—a faith, an ideology, a religion—that goes far beyond the life of the individual. These beliefs are an essential part of a shared identity. They have a unique power to define—and to divide—us and are a driving force in the politics of much of the world today. Throughout history they have most often been, in the widest sense, religious."[107]

---

[106] *The Zen of Recovery*, 33.
[107] Neil MacGregor, *Living with the Gods: On Beliefs and Peoples*, Alfred A. Knopf, 2018, front flyleaf.

Meditation

Meditation is a useful and important technique for seeking a higher power. Goals for meditation are to calm oneself, to experience quiet and solitude, and to let go of thoughts. The meditator opens himself or herself up to whatever may come as peacefulness develops within the mind and body. In the process one can move from an existence as a "human doing" towards that of a "human being." There are many techniques available that can be learned. No one technique is right for everyone.

A popular and useful technique is mindfulness, derived from Buddhist practice. Mindfulness is a practice in which the meditator quietly gives full attention to the present moment while sitting comfortably and breathing quietly. There are seven attitudes which are thought of as forming the foundation of mindfulness practice. They are non-judging, trusting, beginner's mind, patience, acceptance, non-striving, and letting go. There is considerable overlap within these elements, but the more different ways you can describe the same thing, the better you understand it. An important effect of the practice is shifting from an active thinking mode to a more feeling, intuitive mode, allowing elements from the unconscious to rise to the surface. Breathing techniques are an important component of most meditative practices. Deep breathing is sometimes used, but I prefer shallower quiet breathing that does not develop pressure or tension in the chest. Thinking is the enemy of the meditator, but fighting thoughts just makes it worse. The novice meditator worries that he is doing it wrong, that he should adopt a different practice, that what he is doing is foolish or a waste of time or slips into worry about his life or about a thousand other things. The meditation is rescued from these thoughts by returning to one's breathing, gently focusing attention on the chest, lungs, and heart and letting the thoughts go. It may be necessary to repeat this cycle several times during one meditative session, or to discontinue the session and resume it at another time.

Walking meditation is also very pleasant and sometimes an effective activity in our seeking journey. Finding a quiet place to walk where one can enjoy nature, noticing the sounds, seeing the greenery and wildlife, feeling the sensation of warmth or the breeze on one's skin can enhance one's spirit and open one up to possibly finding a higher power. Cold weather also offers unique opportunities such as cross-county skiing and snowshoeing for quiet communion with nature. Troubling thoughts may appear and can be released by focusing on the immediate experience of nature's sights and sounds. Some people may enjoy listening to music (see) as they walk.

Another meditative practice is quietly working on hobbies: gardening, practicing a musical instrument, working on a collection of something, knitting, or many other activities that can be pursued in an almost mindless, automatic way allowing the mind to relax and release worry and tension. Most religions have meditation practices for the believer to try. For example, in the Christian religion we find saying a rosary, entering a labyrinth, and stations of the cross as methods of meditation. By relaxing through meditation, a person can open a channel that allows an experience of a higher power to enter one's consciousness. It is seeking by letting go.

The Wisdom of Others

Howard Thurman

"There is very great virtue in the cultivation of silence, and strength to be found in using it as a door to God."[108]

Jon Kabat-Zinn

"We practice mindfulness by remembering to be present in all our waking moments."[109]

---

[108] Howard Thurman, *Meditations of the Heart*, Beacon Press, 1953,1981, 18.
[109] Jon Kabat-Zinn, *Full Catastrophe Living: Using the Wisdom of Your Body and Mind to Face Stress, Pain, and Illness*, Delta, 1990, 29.

Michael Cowl Gordon

Mystery

Mystery refers to a situation or circumstance that is not fully explainable, at least, not at the time that it is being considered. The term is applied to a genre of fiction in which the reader finds the characters in situations that only at the end of the book become fully understandable. There are spy novels, murder mysteries, tales of lost treasure, and other such types of stories. Or a mystery could be a question that someone has about their world, about life, about why certain things are the way they are.

One mystery that everyone confronts in life has to do with the idea of God. Some people are uncomfortable with God as a mystery, and therefore they seek specific answers. Many such people find an answer that satisfies them to the point that the mystery is essentially solved. They adopt a belief system that informs them of who God is, what God expects of them, and what their reward will be if they obey what they believe to be God's directives. Other people's discomfort is more with the specific answers they encounter, such as the dogma of organized religions. Such people are more comfortable with leaving the Ultimate as a mystery. They think that no one answer could possibly be right for everyone. They believe that truth in this sense cannot be absolute. This idea works only if God is ultimately believed to be unknowable. In this circumstance, what is true for one person may not be true for the next. In the process of seeking a higher power it is important to decide whether you need specific answers to who or what the higher power is, or whether it is better for you to leave it unresolved. It is also okay to reach a conclusion, but to later change your mind. As you have new life experiences you may be influenced in a new direction or belief. I think it is important to be comfortable with the notion that your truth may not be your neighbor's truth. Having respect for the path of other seekers of the truth is key to your own peace of mind, and a safeguard against the arrogance of being certain that you are right and knowing more than people with whom you disagree.

Mysticism

Mysticism is a way of reaching beyond the rational, and it can be thought of as intuitive knowledge of spiritual things, as contrasted with book knowledge of traditional lore. Forms of mysticism and esoteric thought can be found in most if not all religions. It is a response to the understanding that God cannot be thought of exactly as God is. For example, the thirteenth century Christian mystic, Meister Eckhart wrote, "God's nothingness fills the entire world; his something though is nowhere." This calls to mind the Native American expression that God is a circle whose center is everywhere, but its circumference is nowhere. Such paradoxical expressions cause us to expand our consciousness and ways of thinking as we try to approach the idea of God, or if you prefer, a higher power. Despite the presence of mystical elements in religion, many religions seek to suppress the experience, relying instead on "salvation" through adherence to doctrinal beliefs. As I have walked my own journey through life, I have been increasingly attracted to elements that seem to exist beyond the rational. Many writers and spiritual people I quote and refer to in this book are mystics, yet come from widely divergent traditions: Rabbi Heschel, Dr. Jung, Joseph Campbell, Black Elk, Thomas Merton, and many others. I am convinced through their influence as well as my own experiences that there is more than I can ever know about the higher power. I absolutely prefer leaving the Ultimate as a mystery.

Religion

Religion is a term that ordinarily refers to a body of beliefs in and manner of worship of a specific deity. More broadly, it can refer to a deep belief in or devotion to almost anything, for example, baseball or music. We will limit our consideration of religion, though, to belief systems that relate to a higher power. In the United States in 2024, religion is an important part of the lives of a significantly fewer number of people than it was ten years ago. According to reporting by Mike Allen on Mar 29, 2024, in Axios, a new survey by the nonpartisan Public Religion Research Institute (PRRI) found that 26% of Americans now consider themselves unaffiliated with a religion — 5 points higher than 2013. Just a slim majority of Americans (53%) now say religion is important in their lives, down from 72% in 2013.

Roman Catholics are seeing the largest decline in affiliation of any religious group. In 2023, 18% of white Americans said they grew up as Catholics. But one-third of these people said they no longer identify as members of their childhood faith. Twelve percent of Hispanic Americans said they grew up as Catholics. One-third of them also said they no longer identify as such. The percentage of Americans who identify as white evangelical Protestants appears to have stabilized after years of decline. Black Protestants and Jewish Americans have the highest retention rates of all religious groups. For some people religion seems to be little more than an insurance policy. They attend worship services and give lip service to a belief, just in case the teachings happen to be true.[110]

Rabbi Rami Shapiro in his book, *Holy Rascals*, says it is better to categorize religions as healthy or unhealthy rather than true or false. He says the healthy religions "are about universal wisdom and love, about providing meaning in a way that opens your heart, sharpens your mind, and unclenches your fists. Healthy religion invites you to meet those of other religions and ask, 'What can I learn from you? Rather than "How can I get you to think like me?"' On the other hand, "unhealthy religions are about power and control, imposing meaning in a manner that inhibits

---

[110] Mike Allen, Axios Daily News Feed, Presented by United for Democracy, March 29, 2024.

questioning, doubt, or learning from those labeled as 'other.' Unhealthy religions worship conformity; are you toeing the line, staying true to tradition, upholding ancient traditions in the name of sacred truths?" Religion can be a spiritual trap when it becomes authoritarian and seeks control or domination over people and institutions. Shapiro rightly says that a religion can have both healthy and unhealthy aspects.[111] A religion can, for example, exhibit great compassion for the less fortunate in our society, and at the same time condemn people for their love interests. I have no right or interest in judging any church, but having said that, if one did make a judgment it could reasonably be on the basis of whether the church is one that would welcome Jesus as he is portrayed in the Gospels; or whether it is a church or synagogue (Jesus was Jewish, after all) that he would consider attending for a meaningful worship experience.

A view expressed by many of the great theologians and philosophers is that it is not possible to comprehend God as God is. There are many examples, starting with the Sanskrit expression," *neti, neti",* meaning "not this, not that." Socrates is quoted as having said that the only fact that he could be certain of is that he knew nothing. The great Jewish philosopher, Maimonides, said that nothing can be said with certainty about God other than "God is." The great German philosopher and theologian, Meister Eckhart said "The highest and loftiest thing that a person can let go of is to let go of God for the sake of God." In other words, it is only by emptying one's mind of all opinions and preconceived ideas that we can make room for the Truth. And St. Augustine, Father Ed Dowling (Bill Wilson's sponsor), and many others have pointed out that if you can name it, if you can describe it, it's not God.

Many people will find that their needs for a sense of belonging and purpose are found and satisfied within the rooms and relationships of Alcoholics Anonymous or other twelve-step fellowship. For others, they experience after some time in the program that they want or need more. They find that their connection with a higher power is not fully met or satisfied. For many such people, seeking a higher power through

[111] Rami Shapiro, *Holy Rascals: Advice for Spiritual Revolutionaries*, 2017, 35. Used with permission of the publisher, Sounds True, Inc.

religious observance is a viable pathway. Most such people will seek a religious affiliation, not as a substitute for their twelve-step group, but as a supplement to it. Many will return to the religion of their childhood. They may find the worship services, rituals, and music comforting and meaningful in a way that escaped them as children or young adults. Or they may revisit their childhood religion and fail to find what they are looking for in the way of a spiritual experience or higher power. Others will seek out a new denomination within the religion of their childhood. Still others will explore an entirely new approach, such as coming from a Jewish background and exploring Buddhism or Christianity. A point worth making is that it is the search itself that matters the most and will produce the closest thing to the finding of a higher power. It is something like dancing. In dancing it is the movement around the dance floor itself, the experiencing of the music and one's dance partner in the process that brings about enjoyment and satisfaction. The spot where you wind up on the dance floor when the music stops is of no consequence whatsoever.

One of the chief benefits of religion is having a sense of connection, of belonging, of being loved and accepted. This sense of belonging is also a major benefit of involvement in AA or another twelve-step group. A barrier for some AA members regarding attending services of a church can be not feeling understood or accepted. They may believe their history with alcohol may be viewed as sinful by the church members and even by the clergy. Feeling judged in this way will not be helpful. Rabbi Harold Kushner wrote that "Religion is not first and foremost a series of teachings about God. Religion is first and foremost the community through which you learn to understand the world and grow to be human."[112]

MCG – I love this, and it is in this sense only that a twelve-step fellowship can be understood as a religion.

---

[112] *Who Needs God?* 197.

The Wisdom of Others

Rabbi Rami Shapiro

"Once you realize that every religion is making the same claim as Coke— 'It's the real thing'—you cannot help but realize that, like Coke, every religion is filled with fizz."[113]

MCG – This is amusing, but probably unfair. It may only be true of religions that believe that not only are they right, but that every other belief system is wrong.

The Dalai Lama:

"There is no need for temple or church, for mosque or synagogue, no need for complicated philosophy, doctrine, or dogma. Our own heart, our own mind, is the temple. The doctrine is compassion."[114]

George Carlin

"Tell people there's an invisible man in the sky who created the universe, and the vast majority will believe you. Tell them the paint is wet, and they have to touch it to be sure." [115]

MCG - A reason that people believe that the universe was created by God is because God as Creator is an archetype. An archetype is a motif or symbol. Jung (see) wrote that archetypes are carried in the collective unconscious.

---

[113] *Holy Rascals*, 8.
[114] The 14th Dalai Lama, *Our Own Heart Is the Temple*. www.justdharma.org, August 25, 2023.
[115] George Carlin. www.goodreads.com/quotes.

Archbishop William Temple

"It is a great mistake to suppose that God is only, or even chiefly, concerned with religion."[116]

Duane Bidwell

"If religion is an experience rather than a set of beliefs, all sorts of things become possible."[117]

Brother David Steindl-Rast

"The quest of the human heart for meaning is the heartbeat of every religion."[118]

---

[116] Archbishop William Temple, www.episcopal.cafe/William_temple_2/.
[117] *When One Religion Isn't Enough*, 75.
[118] Brother David Steindl-Rast, www.gratefulness.org, Word for the Day, January 31, 2024.

Prayer

Prayer is another topic about which countless things have been written and preached. In one way of thinking, prayer makes sense only if one has already found one's higher power. Then the prayer is directed towards a specific god, saint, or entity. What sense does it make to pray if a person has no idea if someone is paying attention, listening, or has any concern about the person who is trying to make contact? However, experience has shown that there is value in praying anyway. As the Jewish philosopher Martin Buber wrote, "In our prayers themselves God lets Himself be found."[119] If this is so, then the attempt is more than worthwhile.

Prayer can be generated both in the mind and in the heart. There are all kinds of prayers. Prayers of thanksgiving are commonly recited, often sincerely, even if we don't know to whom exactly we should be grateful. There are "foxhole prayers," prayers of desperation to get out of a dangerous situation. There are the "God, this is your last chance "prayers. I know several people who asked for a sign so that they would not kill themselves. One such (true) story is told in my book, *The Twelve Step Pathway: A Heroic Journey of Recovery.* One night Niall was on the verge of driving his car off a cliff and ending it all, but after parking the car, he got out and told God that he had one last chance to send him a sign. A few seconds later, a car parked near him and the couple in the car proceeded to make love. Niall laughed, took it as a sign, and the crisis passed.[120]

Most people think of praying as asking for something. Someone is sick, or there is a financial crisis—no money for food or rent, or on the verge of losing one's life savings. People at various times feel unable to accomplish something and hope that a prayer will be answered. At other times God is worshipped. People tell God how wonderful God is. It is hard to imagine that God is so vain that God will be responsive to or requires flattery; but these prayers of worship are for the benefit of the one who prays, often

---

[119] *Hasidism and Modern Man*, 192.
[120] Michael Cowl Gordon, *The Twelve Step Pathway: A Heroic Journey of Recovery*, Rowman & Littlefield, 2023, 63.

said in the company of a community, and serving to solidify their bonds with each other.

It is reasonable to suppose there are certain things that the higher power cannot do. For example, I don't believe that God can force me to love God, or that if God could do so it would mean anything. I find it helpful to think of the higher power as wanting to connect with people. The higher power sends out signals, and people hopefully will notice these signals and respond to them. In fact, one of the signals could be the desperate loneliness and powerlessness that people feel at certain times in their lives.

To some people the idea of an all-powerful higher power creates a serious obstacle to belief. If God is all-powerful, why are innocent people allowed to suffer? This concept makes people either disbelieve in God or hate God. But what if God suffers along with us? In that case an effective prayer would be to have compassion for God. We all know what it is like to be scorned and unloved, to be in pain. It is sometimes useful to try to view the world from the viewpoint of a higher power rather than from our own self-centered perspective.

A prayer typically recited at the start of the day by an observant Jew is the *Modeh Ani* prayer. I write about it here because it identifies certain characteristics of a higher power that I find helpful. Possibly you will as well; or if not, you may at least give these attributes some consideration. While I am by no means observant, nevertheless I find this prayer to be helpful in my daily seeking of a higher power, and I start each day with it. The full translation reads, "I stand before you, living and eternal King. With compassion you have restored my soul to me. Great is your faithfulness." At the start of the prayer, I present myself to my higher power. For me this means that today I will try to live my life according to the will of my higher power. The word *modeh* (I stand) comes from the same root as *todah*, which means thanks. So, there is the additional meaning of presenting myself in thanksgiving to my higher power. I experience gratitude to my higher power for our relationship. The prayer makes the point that the higher power is alive and eternal, that is, not limited by time. It refers to the higher power as "King," a designation that I do not care for. Human kings can be cruel, arbitrary, dispense justice unequally, conscript young men to fight in their wars, and can levy burdensome taxes. I choose to believe that my higher power is benevolent; therefore, in my translation for myself I substitute the term God for King. It goes on to credit the higher power for maintaining my soul with compassion. Elsewhere in this book I have made the point that it is useful to think of the soul (see) as a point of intersection or concurrence with the higher power. The last statement about the higher power relates to its faithfulness. I take this to mean committed to a relationship with me and is a statement that the higher power has a direct interest in me, personally. People may disagree with each of these statements about a higher power, but as I have advised elsewhere, you might as well seek a higher power that you like. I have done so.

The Wisdom of Others

Alcoholics Anonymous

"We shouldn't be shy on this matter of prayer. Better men than we are using it constantly. It works if we have the proper attitude and work at it."[121]

Harold Kushner

"Prayer, when it is offered in the right way, redeems people from isolation. It assures them that they need not feel alone and abandoned. It lets them know that they are a part of a greater reality, with more depth, more hope, more courage, and more of a future than any individual could have by himself."[122]

---

[121] *Alcoholics Anonymous*, 85-86.
[122] Harold Kushner, *When Bad things Happen to Good People*, Avon Books, 1981, 121.

Adin Steinsaltz

"We can compare the need to pray with the feeling of hunger."[123]

Twelve Steps and Twelve Traditions

"Prayer and meditation are our principal means of conscious contact with God."[124]

"Those of us who have come to make regular use of prayer would no more do without it than we would refuse air, food, or sunshine."[125]

Sam Shoemaker

"Prayer, mind you, is not an effort to affect the will of God but to discover it."[126]

MCG – Rev. Sam Shoemaker was the rector of Calvary Episcopal Church in New York City during the time that Bill Wilson got sober and was starting the AA program. Calvary was at that time also the headquarters of the Oxford Movement. At first, Bill attended Oxford Group meetings until he was able to separate from them and hold meetings independently. Shoemaker was able to provide tremendous encouragement and support to the AA group, so much so that Bill Wilson credited him with being a co-founder of Alcoholics Anonymous.

---

[123] Adin Steinsaltz, *The Thirteen Petalled Rose: A Discourse on the Essence of Jewish Existence & Belief,* Maggid Books, Expanded Edition, 1996, 100.
[124] *Twelve Steps and Twelve Traditions,* 96.
[125] Ibid., 97.
[126] Helen Smith Shoemaker, *I Stand by the Door: The Life of Sam Shoemaker,* Word Books, 1967, 40.

Dr. Bob and the Good Oldtimers

Upon a request for a prayer for himself from a prospective new patient, Sister Ignatia responded, "I will indeed, but pray for yourself as well. There's nothing God likes to hear more than a strange voice."[127]

Andy F.

"If you are an agnostic and will try prayer, I assure you that you will also find an effective higher power in prayer. It is unnecessary to believe in God for prayer to be an effective recovery tool. It is a demonstration of a daily surrender to the actions that need to be taken to recover. This requires some humility. It is also a power greater than us. Prayer is also an affirmation that alcoholism is an illness that is more powerful than us. By surrendering daily to the futility of life run on self-will, prayer is good insurance against ego-driven mistakes, leading to failure. Praying as an agnostic is merely an affirmation of an intention."[128]

"We may wonder what we are praying to. Is anyone listening? When we pray, *we are listening.* Prayer is a direct communication with the healthy part of us that agreed to get sober in the first place. Prayer subdues the inner dialogue of the negative ego."[129]

Anne Lamott

"When you pray, you are not starting the conversation from scratch, just remembering to plug back into a conversation that's always in progress."[130]

"'Help' is a prayer that is always answered. It doesn't matter how you pray...Some people think that God is in the details, but I have come to believe that God is in the bathroom. Prayer usually means praise, or

---

[127] *Dr. Bob and the Good Oldtimers*, Alcoholics Anonymous World Services, Inc., 1980, 192.
[128] *The Twelve Steps for Agnostics*, 136-137.
[129] Ibid., 137.
[130] *Plan B*, 25.

surrender, acknowledging that you have run out of bullets. But there are no firm rules. As Rumi wrote, 'There are hundreds of ways to kneel and kiss the ground.'"[131]

Ralph Waldo Emerson

"Prayer is the contemplation of the facts of life from the highest point of view."[132]

---

[131] Ibid., 37.

[132] Ralph Waldo Emerson, https://libquotescom/ralph-waldo-emerson/.

The Bible and Other Sacred Writings

Many religions base their beliefs and practices on sacred writings that guide their understanding of who or what God is, and how they are supposed to behave. Some religious groups believe that their sacred texts were directly given by God to their founders—that they are literally the word of God. Other religions have sacred texts that they believe are God-inspired. Still others don't have a traditional Western idea of God yet do have sacred writings they believe to carry great wisdom. Yet other religions have no texts at all. Whether you do or do not believe that the Bible is the word of God will have a significant effect on your search for a higher power. Indeed, people who do believe that the Bible is the word of God may well be satisfied that their search is over, and that they have found their higher power.

For those for whom such things are more mysterious, there is nevertheless much worthwhile to be gleaned from the Bible or other sacred writings. These texts typically consist of stories, laws, poems in praise of God, wisdom texts such as epistles and aphorisms, and prophetic writings, and much wisdom can be found within their pages. Nevertheless, the original texts are ancient, and in many cases have not survived intact. What we have are copies written by scribes. What we mostly have are copies of copies of copies, etc. In the process of executing such transcriptions at least four kinds of errors may occur. First, the copy over time may become hard or impossible to read, leaving the next scribe to use his best judgment about what a letter or word may be. Secondly, a simple error in transcription may occur, and then this error becomes established as subsequent copies are made. Third, the scribe may deliberately alter the text in order to emphasize the scribe's own beliefs, or to de-emphasize the beliefs of past priests or scribes. Finally, the actual meaning of a word in its original language may be lost or misinterpreted.

When in the West we talk about the Bible we can generally agree on what books we are discussing, except that the exact understanding of what the Bible is will depend upon a person's religion. Not all Christian denominations agree on exactly which books should be included in the

Bible. For Jewish people the Bible is referred to as the Tanach, consisting of three sections: the Torah (Five Books of Moses), the Prophets, and the Writings. For Christians these books comprise what we can call the Hebrew Bible. Christians also refer to the Hebrew Bible as the Old Testament. The remainder of the Christian Bible is called the New Testament. It is comprised of the Gospels, Acts of the Apostles, Epistles, and the Book of Revelation. Even within the Christian religion there is no consensus on which books are sacred. For example, the Book of Mormon is considered God-given by the Church of Jesus Christ of Latter-day Saints (the LDS Church, or Mormons.) Among Jews there is a wealth of post-Biblical writings, including the Talmud, which for some factions carry as much authority as the Tanach itself. I believe there is much of value to be gained from looking through sacred writings, whether one reads the Bible, the Quran, the Bhagavad Gita, the Upanishads, the Te Tao Ching, or whatever such text you may have at your disposal. It is too easy for some people to discount such books as nonsense because they find stories such as the first story in the book of Genesis in which an important character is a talking snake. I believe if such books are approached respectfully, and with an open mind, there is much that can be learned that will assist seekers of a higher power.

The Wisdom of Others

Richard Rohr

"Without the Spirit, Bible study does not lead to divine intimacy and union; rather, it can lead to self-sufficiency and confirmation about why we're right. Instead of leading us to God, it becomes a way for us to protect ourselves and to judge and diminish other people."[133]

---

[133] Richard Rohr's Daily Meditations, meditations@cac.org., *Life in the Spirit: Weekly Summary*, Saturday, May 25, 2024.

Creation

Man is a thinking being unlike, for example, a squirrel that as far as we can determine, never wonders where its world came from, or what it means to be a squirrel. In our noticing ourselves and the world, we wonder how this all came about and what it means. In terms of where and how the universe came to be it seems that two possibilities exist, although there may be more. The world either had a beginning or it has always just existed. The lack of an origin of the world seems implausible, and science has gathered evidence that the universe is expanding, suggesting that it originated at a single point. If we accept the concept of a beginning, then we are motivated to try to understand how this could have happened. As marvelous and complex as the universe is, it seems more than likely that there was a creative force involved in the formation of the world. Most if not all indigenous tribes have creation myths. These deal with both the origin of the world and the origin of their particular tribe. Joseph Campbell (see) made mythology his life's work, and he wrote extensively about these stories. The Hebrew Bible has such a story—two variations, in fact. The Bible has God creating the world and placing man and woman therein. Somewhat later in the book the narrative deals with the particular place of the Hebrew people in God's plan.

The creation of the universe looks like a massive undertaking requiring 1) power; 2) intelligence; and 3) purpose. Fulfilling these criteria appears to many people to require a super-rational supreme being. We wonder about these things and arrive at our own conclusions based on the stories explaining these questions that we find in our own traditions as well as relying on our own intuition. While some religions teach their beliefs about the exact who, what, and why of the supreme being, generally referred to as God, many thinking people conclude that given the limits of their own mind, it is not possible to think about God as God is. Nevertheless, thousands of very smart people have devoted their lives to the study of theology and have written books expressing their views.

For those who come to believe in a Creator it shouldn't be that difficult to believe that as part of the created universe, we are the objects of intention of the higher power. It can begin to make sense that the higher power seeks a relationship with each of us, and if we open ourselves and embark on the journey the higher power will assist us in our search.

The understanding of Creation in Eastern religions differs from that of the West. There is no mention of a supreme deity that created the world in Eastern religions. For Westerners, the idea that the world was not created by an all-powerful God is hard to grasp. Instead, in the East the creative energy is seen as originating in what is referred to as the Void, or Emptiness. The Void is possibly most understandable in the concept of Ch'i, a Taoist belief. In Taoism, Ch'i is the ground substance of existence, the breath of life. When Ch'i consolidates, matter is formed, and eventually such matter dissolves back into Ch'i. The origin of Ch'i is not dealt with, as far as I understand, just as in Western religion, the origin of God is not addressed. Here we have a remarkable similarity with the view of Albert Einstein, who stated that matter is consolidation from the field, and that the field is the only reality. This corresponds to the Buddhist idea of the non-permanence of things.

Many people have come to believe and teach that God is Love, that Love itself is a creative power—that creation was and still is an act of Love. The question I asked myself years ago was, "If God is Love, did not God need a love object?" If so, then creation is the inevitable solution to God's loneliness. When my daughter was in her mid-teens, I told her that God had created the world because God was lonely. This thought was stored in her mind. As a college student she took a course, an introduction to African American literature. One day she read a collection of poems by James Weldon Johnson entitled *God's Trombones: Seven Negro Sermons in Verse*. One of the poems is entitled *The Creation*. Here are the first few lines, which I have already quoted in an earlier section of this book.

> "And God stepped out in space,
> And he looked around and said:
> I'm lonely—
> I'll make me a world."[134]

---

[134] *God's Trombones: Seven Negro Sermons in Verse*, 15.

And my daughter said to herself, "Hmm, Daddy was right."

This is a nice little story. It satisfies me as to the "why" of creation, but I freely admit that it is only true for me, not necessarily true for others. The conclusion most people in the West come to is that the universe is a created entity, and that creation itself was brought about by a higher power typically referred to as God. So, the world itself is the best argument for the existence of God, according to this logic. But each of you must draw your own conclusions.

Atheism

"Is God willing to prevent evil, but not able? Then he is impotent. Is he able, but not willing? Then he is malevolent. Is he both able and willing? Then whence cometh evil? Is he neither able nor willing? Then why call him God?"[135]

Epicurus (341-270 BCE)

Atheists are people who believe that there is no God, that there is no transcendent being who created the world, placed mankind in it, loves us, tests us, judges us, and reserves a place for us in heaven or hell. They believe the idea of God is illogical, defying reason. They see evil in the world causing suffering that they believe is incompatible with the existence of a loving, all-powerful God. Likewise, they don't believe in evil as a transcendent force presided over by an evil being, commonly referred to as Satan, or the Devil. For atheists, the world is entirely as it appears to be to our rational mind. Nevertheless, they typically believe in the importance of ethics, justice, and morality, but deny that such values are important or have authority because of imposition by a higher power.

Some religions, for example, Buddhism (see), don't have a theology that includes a Western idea of God. The Buddha himself refused to say whether he believed or disbelieved in God. And when asked if he was a god he denied this, saying only, "I am awake." There are other religions as well where the belief in a deity is not part of the religious philosophy. This is true of Jainism and other groups, primarily found in the East. However, one can easily find atheists who belong to various Western denominations including Judaism, Christianity, and the Unitarian Universalist church.

To some, the idea of atheism as a philosophy makes no sense, because it is a statement of non-belief rather than belief in something. For example, there is no specific word for a category of people who do not believe that there is a workshop at the North Pole manned by elves and presided over by an old reindeer herder who wears a red suit. Einstein himself said that

---

[135] Goodreads.com/quotes/8199-is-god-willing-to-prevent-evil-but-not-able-then.

atheism is no philosophy at all. Nevertheless, a seemingly logical argument can be made in favor of atheism (see above quote of Epicurus).

Many writers argue against the existence of God because of the atrocities committed in the name of religion. These atrocities include the Crusades, the Inquisition, the burning of witches, and terrorist attacks. Christopher Hitchens has catalogued these crimes against humanity extensively in his book, *god Is Not Great*. Others believe that one cannot condemn God or deny the existence of a deity based on the actions of humans. In fact, some of the worst atrocities in history have been committed, justified not by religion, but by non-theistic ideology. The examples of the imprisonment and slaughter of millions of people by communist regimes in Russia (Stalin) and China (Mao Zedong) and the Nazi regime in Germany (Hitler) come to mind all too easily.

Various surveys have been conducted to determine the percentage of people in society that consider themselves to be atheists. According to the American Family Survey,[136] 34% were found to be religiously unaffiliated in 2017 (23% 'nothing in particular', 6% agnostic, 5% atheist). This is typical of most surveys in the United States where the percentage of people who consider themselves to be atheists is around 5%, with a somewhat higher percentage calling themselves agnostic (see). In Europe these percentages vary wildly, depending upon the country surveyed. According to the 2010 Eurobarometer Poll[137], the percentage of those polled who agreed with the statement "you don't believe there is any sort of spirit, God or life force" varied from a high percentage in France (40%), down to the Czech Republic (37%), Sweden (34%), Netherlands (30%), Estonia (29%), Germany (27%), Belgium (27%), UK (25%); to very low in Poland (5%), Greece (4%), Cyprus (3%), Malta (2%), and Romania (1%), with the European Union as a whole at 20%. In a 2012 Eurobarometer poll on discrimination in the European Union,[138] 16% of those polled considered themselves non-believers/agnostics, and 7% considered themselves atheists.

---

[136] American Family Survey, Deseret News, December 6, 2017.
[137] Special Eurobarometer: Biotechnology, October 2010, 381.
[138] Special Eurobarometer, 383, *Discrimination in the EU in 2012*, European Union: European Commission, 2012, 233.

Some famous people are known to have been atheists. Karl Marx called religion "the sigh of the oppressed creature, the heart of a heartless world, and the soul of soulless conditions. It is the opium of the people".[139] Voltaire believed that society required law and order, and that people would only follow laws willingly if they believed they were imposed by a deity or higher power. For this reason, he said that "If God did not exist, it would be necessary to invent him."[140] Plato was of a similar opinion, saying that were it not for fear of divine retribution after death, people would not obey laws or adhere to a social order. In fact, he advocated for locking atheists up.

Many people believe that atheists will have a sudden deathbed conversion as they contemplate the possibility of divine condemnation and punishment for their disbelief. My favorite story in this regard is about Voltaire. When on his deathbed a priest called upon him to renounce the devil and all his works, Voltaire gave his advice consideration but decided not to follow it. "This is no time," he said, "to be making new enemies."

---

[139] Karl Marx, *"Introduction." A Contribution to the Critique of Hegel's Philosophy of Right*, translated by A. Jolin and J. O'Malley, edited by J. O'Malley, Cambridge University Press. – via Marxists, {1843}, 1970.
[140] https://www.brainyquote.com>authors>voltaire-quotes.

Agnosticism

The term "agnosticism" was coined in 1869 by Thomas Henry Huxley, a British biologist and anthropologist, and grandfather of the noted author and philosopher, Aldous Huxley. In its current common usage, it refers to a philosophical position in religion that it is not possible to draw firm conclusions about God from our own experience. More broadly speaking, the term could apply to any topic, religious or otherwise. Huxley said that one should follow one's reason as far as is possible, and once having done so, accept the limits of one's knowledge. It is not a profession of total ignorance. The idea of "not knowing" traces all the way back to Socrates who is supposed to have said that he recognized that he knows nothing at all. An example of not knowing relates to the origin of the universe. A common experience is for people to observe the order and immensity of the universe and assume there is a cause or creator, but not everyone would agree. The philosopher David Hume proposed that one can attribute the order in the universe to the universe itself without requiring an outside cause.

The twelfth century Jewish philosopher Moses Maimonides said that one can only approach an understanding of God by saying what God is not. Thus, he was reduced to a single positive statement about God—that God exists. Any other statement about God can only be preceded by "God is not," and then add whatever descriptor you may wish. This position, called apophatic theology, was endorsed by the thirteenth century Christian theologian, Thomas Aquinas, although he was less extreme in the application of this negative approach. An ancient Sanskrit saying is, "*neti, neti,*" which in reference to the deity means, "not this, not that." In contrast to the proposed failure of logic and empirical experience to lead to a definite conclusion about the deity, religion has recognized that the metaphysical realm contains truths. The German philosopher Emmanuel Kant in his *Critique of Pure Reason* wrote, "I have found it necessary to deny knowledge in order to make room for faith."[141]

---

[141] www.goodreads.com/work/quotes/1072226-kritik-der-reinen-vernunft?page=3.

As a solution to not knowing, seventeenth century French mathematician Blaise Pascal suggested that if one wanted to bet, it would make sense to bet in favor of the Roman Catholic religion, reasoning that life is short, and that eternity is forever. Known as "Pascal's Wager," this solution is unsatisfying in many respects, not the least of which is the Roman Catholic religion is only one of many options available. It also seems to propose a solution based on a desire for self-preservation rather than a search for truth.

Many people who come to AA claim to be agnostic. Their position is one of simply not knowing. They commonly say that they believe in something but can't define what it is. This is a good honest starting place to begin the search. The risk is that it could be accepted as a final position without honestly expending the energy to seek a higher power.

Symbols

A symbol is a representation, usually visual, of something that stands for something else. The value of a symbol is that it can elicit a feeling or sense of something that is beyond the ordinary. Symbols can help people to think more deeply about something—to be emotionally moved—to have an awareness of something beyond. Symbols that represent a group can stimulate a sense of coherence, belonging, importance, and loyalty. The logo is used today to stimulate recognition of a company or product. Thus, a picture of a red sign with "Coca-Cola" written in a certain script can elicit a sense of coolness, refreshment, and enjoyment, the slaking of thirst, and for older people a sense of nostalgia. Religions use symbols to help adherents experience a sense of spiritual attachment. Examples are the cross in Christianity and the lotus in Buddhism. Both religions also use statues or pictures of certain religious figures to stimulate deeper thinking, connection, and religious feeling.

To some people a picture is just a picture, the sun and moon are just bodies in the sky, and a mountain is just a mountain. Others are naturally open to being stimulated to see a meaning or experience a feeling beyond and suggested by the physical object. For those whose thinking is more concrete, my suggestion is to try to allow yourselves to be open to the "seeing beyond" that others experience. Joseph Campbell (see) used to say that those who cannot see beyond the symbols are like people who go to a restaurant and eat the menu. And according to the Jungian scholar Murray Stein, "A symbol attracts a great deal of energy to itself and shapes the ways in which psychic energy is channeled and spent."[142] As always, in seeking a higher power we need to be aware that it is we who create the obstacles to progress along spiritual lines.

Crossing a river is symbolic of making a major change in one's life, attitude, or sense of purpose. Likewise, passing through a doorway also can represent such a major step. It is a threshold experience. Entering a cave or otherwise experiencing total darkness can represent the descent into a deep sadness or aloneness in one's life; or, it can represent a descent

---

[142] Murray Stein. *Jung's Map of the Soul.* Open Court, 81.

into hell. Religious symbols such as the wine and bread of the Christian Eucharist symbolize unity and transformation, enabling the recipient to transition from the ordinary to the sublime. Each of us is on his or her own journey, and the symbols we encounter will affect us uniquely. Here are a few of the symbols we might encounter in our daily lives, and a bit of information of what they have represented to others.

The sky.

The sky is commonly seen as a source of life in a masculine way and sometimes referred to as Father Sky. It inspires us with its beauty and vastness and with all that we see in its expanse: the sun, moon, stars, comets, clouds, rain, rainbows. The sky is changeable, changing colors, weather patterns, and transitioning between day and night. We have eclipses that are awe-inspiring, that increase our awareness of the remarkable universe in which we live. Deeper imaging of the universe reveals billions of galaxies, astonishing distances, dark matter, black holes, various categories of stars, and much more. When we think of heaven, of God, we look up at the sky. Not that we necessarily think that God is "up there" as opposed to anywhere else, but it is our natural inclination to look upwards to find a spiritual source. Light symbolizes understanding and goodness, whereas darkness can symbolize confusion and evil.

The sun.

The sun is the most powerful object in our part of the world. People have always recognized their dependence upon the sun for life itself, and there is a long history of sun worship. Another characteristic of the sun is its regularity, both in its daily behavior, and in the marking of the seasons. The sun is incorporated in countless myths, typically portrayed as masculine as opposed to the feminine imagining of the moon. The sun plays a role in the oldest recorded story that we have, Gilgamesh, where the hero Gilgamesh, king of Uruk, journeys to the garden of the sun seeking immortality. While in our society today practically nobody actually worships the sun, we are aware of our absolute dependence upon the sun for our very existence, and of our powerlessness to affect the sun in any way.

The moon

The moon is the most prominent celestial body in the night sky, by far. From the standpoint of astronomy, it is remarkably close to the earth, so close that its gravitational force causes oceanic tides. It is the subject of countless myths, generally taking on a feminine persona in contrast to the sun. It is admired for its beauty. Mythologic names include Selene, Artemis, and Luna, among many others. Like people, the moon has a dark side. It has been either worshipped or incorporated into worship services for thousands of years and is depended upon to mark the passage of time. Traditionally, for example, in the Jewish religion the observance of the holidays specified in the Torah is tied to the phases of the moon, and every month the new moon is recognized with special prayers.

Earth

Unlike the sky which is "up there," the earth is "down here." It represents groundedness, stability, nurturing, and is typically viewed as feminine—Mother Earth. All life as we know it is found on the earth, and the life force is referred to as Mother Nature. Cultures that live close to nature are inspired spiritually by all the living and inanimate things that exist on earth, attributing sanctity to the plants, streams, mountains, and the animals encountered. The need for food has inspired spiritual and religious beliefs as communities depended upon hunting, gathering, and agriculture for their survival. Despite the nurturing sense about the earth, it is also a dangerous place where groups are at risk of experiencing flooding, drought, earthquakes, volcanoes, extreme heat or cold, diseases, attack by wild animals, and attack by other groups of people. There are spaces on earth where one might have a more spiritual experience. I had such an experience the first time I visited a redwood forest in California. Each of us can find a sacred space if we are open and paying attention.

Fire

Fire often is seen as symbolizing change—both destruction and regeneration. From the ashes rises the Phoenix. Fire also symbolizes light, illuminating the darkness of ignorance and fear. Fire is used in purification rituals and in refining ore. Fire is used in healing, both in rituals as well as in cautery as used in modern medicine. Fire is a necessity in preparing food, and as such is a participant in the life force in human existence. Fire is an important symbol in some religious observances. The Zoroaster religion maintains a fire that has been burning continuously for well over two thousand years. In the Jewish religion an oil lamp was kept perpetually burning in the Temple. Now synagogues typically have a representation of this fire, whether gas, oil, or electric, prominently displayed near the ark that contains the Torah scrolls. In Greek mythology fire was the possession of Zeus, the chief God. It symbolized knowledge, civilization, and creativity. Prometheus was a lesser God who stole the fire from Zeus and gave it to mankind. In punishment, Zeus fastened Prometheus to the side of a mountain where an eagle came daily to devour his liver which regenerated eternally. Fire holds visual fascination for people as it flickers, roars, and gives off sparks. As a symbol of illumination, regeneration, purification, healing, and in being visually fascinating, fire offers a useful symbol for "seeing beyond."

Water

Water is, along with air, the most vital source of life. Water can symbolize purity as it cleanses. This cleansing aspect is seen in the Christian rite of Baptism, where sins are washed away, and the soul is purified. In psychology, water symbolizes the unconscious, which is seen as vast and mysterious as the ocean. Mystically, water represents spirituality. By its ability to take many forms water symbolizes change.

In Islam, water symbolizes purification, birth, life, and healing. Washing with water precedes ritual prayers. In the Jewish religion, ritual hand washing is done before meals. In the Hindu religion, water is a symbol of spiritual cleansing and purification. Bathing in the Ganges River is spiritually healing, and the souls of those cremated by the river are thought to be advanced to heaven.

Tree

The tree is a special symbol because it connects the earth with the sky. Thus, it symbolizes unity. Certain trees are sacred to certain religious groups. The cottonwood is sacred to the Lakota Sioux, and the banyan tree is sacred to Hindus. In the Bible trees figure importantly in the creation stories. One tree contained the secret of life, and another the secret knowledge of good and evil. Trees symbolize life as they give off oxygen, provide nesting places for birds and other animals, and provide shelter.

Heaven and Hell

Everything I have written in this manuscript is my own opinion, so please take it as opinion as opposed to fact. For that matter, everything anyone says about heaven and hell seems to me to be opinion as opposed to fact. But that is just my opinion. Even the quotes I have included from other people are just their opinions, although since I have included them here, they are worthy of deep consideration, in my opinion.

As far as heaven and hell are concerned, this is what makes sense to me. For many of us, hell is created for us right here on earth by cruel circumstances. We experience such hell entirely as victims as children, when we may be subjected to sickness, slavery, hunger, sexual, physical, and emotional abuse, tribal or national warfare, gangs, lack of sanitation, imprisonment, exposure to the elements, and other such horrors. All these miseries and more can be part of our adult lives as well. Whatever hellish conditions that we may be subjected to by the circumstances of our lives over which we have no control may not compare with the hell that we subject ourselves to through giving in to drugs, alcohol, or the myriad other ways we may become addicted. So, I believe that hell is right here on earth.

What about those who say that we may be subjected to a hellish existence in an afterlife, once our breathing stops and we move on to some kind of judgment. Whether there is a final judgment or not, I have no opinion. I would like to think that the people who have enslaved people and killed people by the millions experience some horrible punishment. But I don't really know what to think about this. Most religions address this issue as part of their dogma. They try to scare people into being "good," to avoid this disastrous consequence of wrongful living.

Here is a pithy distinction between religion and spirituality that I have heard. "Religion is for people who are afraid of going to hell, whereas spirituality is for people who have already been there." No doubt this is an oversimplification of things, but there may well be some truth to it. Some religions do strongly emphasize "going to hell" because of not following their directives.

Here is why I have difficulty believing in hell as part of an afterlife. I start with a belief in a higher power that is a force of love. This may or not be the case, but it works for me to believe it. I ask myself how could such a loving force subject the created objects of its love to damnation and eternal torture? It makes no sense. Therefore, there is no hell. This brings us to heaven. About heaven, I am less certain. I would like to believe that there is some sort of pleasant ongoing spiritual existence where we can continue to exist as our distinct selves, but I find this somewhat unconvincing as the reality. What I have decided to do about this is to trust my higher power, who I believe has the whole thing worked out in a better way than I could ever imagine. This is not a cop-out. It is the acceptance of uncertainty in my world. There are certain things that, as Joseph Campbell put it, are beyond the categories of human thought. Among these are higher power (God), eternity, and life after death.

Therefore, I find the concepts of heaven and hell to be completely irrelevant to how I conduct myself as I live my life. If I do the right thing, my motivation is that I do it because it is the right thing to do. If I do the wrong thing, it is because I am human. None of us are perfect, nor are we meant to be. If when I die, I discover myself to be in a certain condition or in a certain manifestation, I hope that I will be able to enjoy and take pleasure in it. Ideally, I will be in a position where I will have the opportunity to be useful in some way. In the meantime, I accept the responsibility to create as much of heaven as possible right here on earth, and the energy I will draw on is love. I hope you can do the same.

Michael Cowl Gordon

Special topics

There is a great deal about religion that I will not write about here. Libraries are full of material on Christianity, Judaism, Islam, and any other religion one could think of. I believe that pursuit of a higher power can be successful through religion, but I can't endorse or urge the following of any one in particular. The choice is up to the seeker to investigate a religion or to become an adherent. Or not. However, I have written on three specific religious paths here because in recent times many people in AA have shown an interest in them. They are Native American Spirituality, Buddhism, and the Jewish spiritual path of Kabbala. I hope it will be helpful to some of my readers to look at these essays. Please consult with other resources for information on these and other religions.

Native American Spirituality – The Red Road

If we define religion as a specific systematic belief in a higher power, or of manner of worship of such higher power; and if we define spirituality as a set of beliefs and practices that relate to the human soul, then while such meanings seem to be related to each other, spirituality comes closer than religion to the relationship of the indigenous First Peoples of the Americas to a higher power. In fact, few if any native languages have a word for religion. According to Vine Deloria, "religion is an experience, and they have no reason to reduce it to systematic thought and the elaboration of concepts."[143] The deity is not represented anthropomorphically in the beliefs of Native American peoples. Furthermore, there is no imperative to engage with the Great Spirit in a personal relationship. Native American people in their spiritual practice are almost constantly engaged in prayer. There is no book in which can be found recorded the stories of their origins, or the laws that their higher power expects them to obey. But there are stories which inform them of their origins, and of their relationship to the higher power. Along with the origin stories there are instructions in ceremonies that the tribes must engage in as a means of remaining in the good graces of their higher power, especially in regard to the continuous provision of food through good hunting, provision of crops through abundant rain, and continuation of the life-blood of the tribe through fertility of the tribe so as to produce children. One such story comes from the Oglala Sioux tribe, who live in the great plains of North America where they are part of the Lakota nation. It is known as the story of the White Buffalo Calf Woman.

One day, a long, long, time ago, two young Sioux men went hunting, and as they proceeded on their way, in the distance they saw a figure approaching. As this figure came nearer, they could see that it was a beautiful young woman who was dressed in white buckskin. They could see that she was carrying a

[143] Vine Deloria, Jr., *God Is Red: A Native View of Religion*, Fulcrum Publishing, 1973, 1992, 2003, 2023, 142.

bundle wrapped in buffalo hide, and when they came close enough, they could hear her singing this song:

> *"Behold me, behold me,*
> *For in a sacred manner, I am walking."*

One of the men recognized that this was a sacred woman, but the other felt lust for her and approached her with sexual intentions. As he reached her, they were enveloped in a white cloud, and when the wind carried the cloud away the respectful Indian saw that his companion was nothing but a pile of bones, crawling with worms. The woman instructed the remaining Indian to return to his village, and to prepare for her arrival by erecting a lodge in which to greet her. They were also instructed to send runners to the other bands of Sioux so that they could all receive instructions directly from her when she came to the village. These things were done, and soon she walked into the lodge, carrying the bundle which contained a sacred object, a pipe. She told them that the Great Spirit, Wakan Tanka, had favored them with this gift. They were to use the pipe in their ceremonies. She explained the symbolism of the pipe. The bowl was carved from red sandstone which represented the earth, their mother, and the ancestors who had died and returned to the dust of the earth. The stem was carved from wood, representing the spirits of the plant world. Twelve spotted eagle feathers hung from the pipe, representing the flying things. Carved into the bowl was the image of a buffalo calf representing the four-leggeds who lived among them. She told them that the pipe was to be used in all their ceremonies, and that it was very sacred and was to be treated with the utmost respect. She then taught them the first ceremony, that of the Keeping of the Soul. She told them that they would learn of six more ceremonies from visions after she had left them and returned to the spirit world. They begged her to stay, but she could not. Amazingly, as she walked away, in the distance they could see that she had been transformed into a white buffalo calf.

While this story contains supernatural elements which makes it difficult to take at face value, this is not so different from stories that seem to be taken as factual by people of other religions. An example might be the Bible story that God created the world, placed the first man in a garden, and because God thought that it was not good for the man to be alone,

He removed one of the man's ribs and from it He fashioned a woman. He instructed the man and the woman not to eat the fruit of a tree that grew in the center of the garden, but a snake spoke to the woman and tricked her into eating the fruit. She in turn, convinced the man to eat the fruit, and for this act of disobedience they were expelled from the garden. Worse, they were marked by the stain of sin which was transmitted to the entirety of the human race which descended from these two people. If there is a difference in these stories, it is that one is written down in a book and the other is not. The details of the stories differ, of course, but whether it is a talking snake or a woman who turns into a buffalo calf, neither fits our expectation of naturally occurring events.

The lives of the people who comprised the First Nations put them into intimate contact with nature. They found themselves within nature, and to them nature extended from the earth and all that dwelled thereupon to the sky, to the sun, the moon, the Milky Way, and the stars. To them, everything was connected to everything else. Their metaphor for this was the circle, one whose center was everywhere, and circumference was nowhere. All existed within the Great Spirit. There are many expressions for this circle. Some called it the Medicine Wheel. For Black Elk it was the Sacred Hoop. In this formulation, everything is sacred. This is why the peoples say that the rivers, the mountains, the forests, the buffalo, and all the land is sacred. The land belonged to them, but more than that, they belonged to the land as a gift of the Great Spirit. The expression in philosophic language for this concept is panentheism. God is in all things, and all things are within God. This differs from pantheism in that with panentheism God is greater than the sum of the universe. There is no limit. (In Kabbala, one of God's names is "Ein Sof – Without Limit.")

Indian formulation of their world emphasizes their sense of place. In ceremony they acknowledge the four directions: North, East, South, and West. Each direction is symbolized by a color, a power, and by a spirit animal. These symbols and colors vary from tribe to tribe. In *Mother Earth Spirituality*, Ed McGaa writes of the symbolism followed by the Oglala Sioux tribe.[144] The color of the North is white, and the spirit animals are

---

[144] Ed McGaa, Eagle Man, *Mother Earth Spirituality*, HarperOne, 1990.

the polar bear, the bald eagle, and the snowy owl. The medicine (power) of the North is Wisdom. The color of the East is red, and the spirit animals are the wolf and the red hawk. The medicines of the East are Illumination and loyalty. The color of the South is yellow, and the spirit animals are the buffalo and the bear. The medicines of the South are prayer, gratitude, and healing. The color of the West is Black, and the spirit animals are the black horse and the Thunderbird. Its medicines are rain and growth. Two additional directions are up, for Father Sky, and down for Mother Earth. Father Sky includes the sky, sun, moon, the "star nations" and the vast expanse. Mother Earth includes all the components of the earth, and all living beings associated with the earth.

Great significance is attached to ceremonies. "Ceremony, to the Indian, is a realization, an experiencing realization of the spirituality that surrounds all. Ceremony brings forth that profound, deeply powerful realization from beyond into the world of the two-leggeds."[145] Ceremony promotes connection to the earth, to the tribe, to the universe, and to *Wakan Tanka*, the Lakota name for the Great Spirit. One such ceremony is called *Hunkapi*, the Making of Relatives. It was established as a way of making peace between different tribes or communities of people. Joseph Epes Brown tells what he learned from Black Elk about this ceremony. "Through these rites a three-fold peace was established. The first peace, which is the most important, is that which comes within the souls of men when they realize their relationship, their oneness, with the universe and with all its Powers, and when they realize that at the center of the universe dwells *Wakan-Tanka*, and that this center is really everywhere, it is within each of us. This is the real Peace, and the others are but reflections of this. The second peace is that which is made between two individuals, and the third is that which is made between two nations. But above all you should understand that there can never be peace between nations until it first known that true peace which, as I have often said, is within the souls of men."[146]

Many non-Indians are attracted to this philosophy and to these ceremonies. Generally speaking, "Playing Indian" is an ill-advised activity.

[145] Ibid., 47.
[146] *The Sacred Pipe: Black Elk's Account of the Seven rites of the Oglala Sioux*, 115.

However, non-Indians can easily find access to a sweat lodge ceremony. Indians and non-Indian people offer such sweat lodge ceremonies to interested or curious people, usually for a fee. While such fee for service ceremonies may lack some of the authenticity and spiritual value of a true indigenous ceremony, it can certainly be instructive about the basics of what a sweat lodge is like. However, there is a possibility for non-Indians to seriously pursue a Native American spiritual path. Such a path would require a teacher and a deep commitment. Interested people should consult Ed McGaa's book, *Rainbow Tribe*. (See Suggested Readings.)

The Wisdom of Others

John (Fire) Lame Deer

"The word for 'prayer' in Lakota is wacekiye, which means 'to claim relationship with' or 'to seek connection to.' To the Lakota people, the cosmos is one family. To live well within the cosmos, one must assume responsibility for everything with which one shares with the universe."[147]

Apache blessing:

"May the sun bring you new energy by day, may the moon softly restore you by night, may the rain wash away your worries, may the breeze blow new strength into your being, and may you walk gently through the world and know its beauty all the days of your life."

Black Elk with John G. Neihardt

As he is relating his great vision to Neihardt, Black Elk says: "And I saw that the sacred hoop of my people was one of many hoops that made one circle, wide as daylight and starlight, and in the center grew one mighty

---

[147] John (Fire) Lame Deer and Richard Erdoes, *Lame Deer: Seeker of Visions*, Washington Square Press, 1972, 1976, 1994, xiv.

flowering tree to shelter all the children of one mother and one father. And I saw that it was holy."[148]

A comment by Neihardt: "Black Elk said the mountain he stood upon in his vision was Harney Peak in the Black Hills. 'But anywhere is the center of the world,' he added."[149]

Ed McGaa, Eagle Man

"Our survival is dependent on the realization that Mother Earth is a truly holy being, that all things in the world are holy and must not be violated, and that we must share and be generous with one another... You must think of Mother Earth as a living being. Think of your fellow men and women as holy people who were put here by the Great Spirit. Think of being related to all things!"[150]

Richard Rohr

Richard Rohr recalls his first experiences with the prayer of the Pueblo people in New Mexico:

"In 1969 when I was a young deacon in Acoma Pueblo, one of my jobs was to take the census. Because it was summer and hot, I would start early in the morning, driving my little orange truck to each residence. Invariably at sunrise, I would see a mother outside the door of her home, with her children standing beside her. She and the children would be reaching out with both hands uplifted to "scoop" up the new day and then "pour" it over their heads and bodies in blessing. I would sit in my truck until they were finished, thinking how silly it was of us Franciscans to think we brought religion to New Mexico four hundred years ago!"[151]

---

[148] Black Elk with John G. Neihardt, *Black Elk Speaks: Being the Life Story of a Holy Man of the Oglala Sioux,* University of Nebraska Press, 1932, 1959, 1961, 1972, 43.

[149] Ibid., 43.

[150] *Mother Earth Spirituality*, 208.

[151] Richard Rohr's Daily Meditations, meditations@cac.org, *Praying with Nature,* Monday, October 30, 2023.

Buddhism and other Eastern religions

In this section I will emphasize Buddhism because for many years many people within the AA program who have sought a higher power have been attracted to Buddhism. Much has been written about other Eastern religions including Hinduism, Jainism, Taoism, Confucianism, and there is no need for me to go into detail about them here. In my section on quantum physics (see), Eastern religions come up, and you will find mention of these ideas there.

The Buddha, Siddhartha Gautama, was born into a wealthy family about 3000 years ago in India. As a young man he led a sheltered existence. He married and had children, but according to the story, at age 29 he went out into the world and discovered how people suffered with poverty, hunger, disease, old age, abandonment, cruelty, exposure to the elements, and neglect. He joined the class of mendicants, beggars who wandered about the countryside, subjecting himself to severe ascetic practices including fasting, other forms of deprivation, and self-inflicted physical pain. After 6 years he had failed to find an answer to his question of why people suffer. One morning he awakened after having fallen asleep under a Bodhi tree, and he had his "awakening." For one thing, he saw that by subjecting himself to extreme practices he had only intensified the focus on himself and his own suffering. He came to understand that the route to enlightenment was the Middle Path, one in which balance is pursued. What the Buddha came to see, as his major insight, was what are now referred to as the Four Noble Truths. These were the Buddha's summary understanding of the causes and the end of suffering and were the subject of his first sermon after his awakening.

The Four Noble Truths comprise the essence of the Buddha's teachings. They are 1) the truth of suffering; 2) the truth of the cause of suffering; 3) the truth of the end of suffering; and 4) the truth of the path that leads to the end of suffering. More simply put, suffering exists; it has a cause; it has an end; and there is a method to bring about its end.

The Four Noble Truths are a plan for dealing with the suffering humanity faces –which includes suffering of a physical, mental, and spiritual nature. According to Buddhism, desire and ignorance lie at the root of suffering. By desire, Buddhists refer to craving pleasure, material goods, and immortality, all of which are wants that can never be satisfied. Because of the fact of impermanence, desiring them can only bring about suffering.

The Third Noble Truth, the truth of the end of suffering, has a dual meaning, suggesting both the end of suffering in this life on earth, and in the spiritual life through achieving Nirvana. Nirvana is a transcendent state of freedom from suffering in which the worldly cycle of birth, death, and rebirth ends because spiritual enlightenment has been achieved.

The Fourth Noble Truth, known to Buddhists as the Noble Eightfold Path, charts the method for attaining the end of suffering. The steps of the Noble Eightfold Path are Right Understanding, Right Thought, Right Speech, Right Action, Right Livelihood, Right Effort, Right Mindfulness and Right Concentration. (Some writers substitute the word "wise" for "right.") Moreover, there are three themes into which the Path is divided: good moral conduct (Understanding, Thought, Speech); meditation and mental development (Action, Livelihood, Effort), and wisdom or insight (Mindfulness and Concentration).

Fundamental to Buddhist understanding is the idea of no-self. This is the understanding that one does not exist in a unique state, separated from the rest of humanity, or indeed, from the rest of the universe, past, present, or future. Thus, as an isolated soul, one is frustrated by whatever is seen to be lacking in one's life, by competitiveness, and by fear of impermanence. As said in the prayer of St. Francis, "it is by self-forgetting that one finds." A phrase in the third step prayer of Alcoholics Anonymous refers to "the bondage of self." It may be more helpful, rather than to think that the self does not exist, to think that it exists only as an entity inseparable from the whole. Think of waves in the ocean or blades of grass on a lawn. The term "yoga" refers to the union or yoking of an individual soul to the souls of others, and to the universal soul, the higher power.

The third Noble Truth is sometimes referred to as the law of dependent origination, and it follows from the idea of no-self. What dependent origination describes is a vision of life or an understanding in which we see the way everything is interconnected—that there is nothing separate, nothing standing alone. Everything affects everything else. We are inseparable from this system. The fundamental axiom of Wise Effort in all cultures and religious traditions is the Golden Rule. We do unto others as we would have them do unto us because in a real sense, they are us, and we are them. There is no absolute separation of souls in the universe. Unity, oneness, is the most fundamental reality. Thus, the saying, "I can't be me without you." The end of suffering can be achieved. Peace is possible, happiness is possible, because peace and happiness in life do not depend on what is going on but rather on how the heart and mind respond to what is happening.

The law of karma is the fourth noble truth. The law of karma is an outgrowth of dependent origination. In one way, karma is a Buddhist religious doctrine that describes various levels of existence, kinds of beings, and the flow of events affecting the dynamics of living within this particular philosophy of life. More commonly in western Buddhism, karma describes cause and effect relationships. What is important to understand is that it only applies to intentional actions. Kindness generates more kindness in the world; love generates more love; selfishness engenders more selfishness; and hate engenders more hate. From a Buddhist point of view, our present mental, moral, intellectual and temperamental differences are, for the most part, due to our own actions and tendencies, both past and present. The notion of "past" includes past lives. The fourth noble truth leads to the conclusion that suffering can be relieved through the practice of the Eightfold Path.

Buddhist practice is designed to bring the individual to a spiritual condition described as a sublime state incorporating four elements: lovingkindness, compassion, sympathetic joy, and equanimity. Thus, for people in recovery the search for a higher power may be conducted by living according to the twelve steps themselves as one develops these personal qualities.

Buddhist teaching is referred to as Dharma, and meditation is the bedrock of Buddhist practice. This is unlike Western religion which emphasizes prayer as the primary means of relating to and accepting and obeying the will of a higher power. The Buddha said such belief in God is irrelevant to the relief of suffering. This is an entirely different way of thinking from the Western approach of praying to God for relief from suffering.

Understanding is the key to Buddhist practice and way of life. According to Buddhist monk Thich Nhat Hanh, "In Buddhism, we speak of salvation by understanding. We see that it is the lack of understanding that creates suffering.... True love is possible only with real understanding. Buddhist meditation—stopping, calming, and looking deeply—is to help us understand better. In each of us is a seed of understanding. That seed is God. It is also the Buddha."[152]

According to Laura S., Wise Understanding provides the individual with the comprehension that he is not simply a victim of fate— that he has choices that can affect the quality and outcome of his life. "Wise understanding consists primarily of the teachings (of) the Four Noble Truths, impermanence, not-self, dependent origination, and karma.... The Buddha.... defined wise thought as 'the thought of renunciation, the thought of non-ill-will, the thought of harmlessness.'" [153]

Buddhist practice requires the understanding of five basic precepts, taken as vows, as the minimum commitment to not harming others through our speech and actions.... These precepts are:

> *"I undertake to refrain from killing and harming living beings.*
> *I undertake to refrain from stealing and taking that which is not mine.*
> *I undertake to refrain from causing harm through sexual misconduct.*
> *I undertake to refrain from false speech, harmful speech, gossip, and slander.*
> *I undertake to refrain from the misuse of intoxicants or substances such as alcohol or drugs that cause carelessness or loss of awareness."*

---

[152] Thich Nhat Hanh, *Living Buddha, Living Christ*, Riverhead Books, 1995, 84.
[153] Laura S., *12 Steps on Buddha's Path: Bill, Buddha, and We*, Wisdom Publications, 2006, 70-71.

It is notable that some of these are found in the Ten Commandments of the Hebrew Bible: Thou shalt not murder, steal, commit adultery, or bear false witness.

Practicing Buddhists 'take refuge' daily in what are known as the Three Jewels or the Three Refuges:

> *"I go for refuge to the Buddha.*
> *I go for refuge to the Dharma.*
> *I go for refuge to the Sangha."*

The Buddha is that state of being awakened – one's "Buddha nature;" It means making the effort to bring mindfulness into each moment. The Dharma is the Buddhist doctrine of the nature of the universe and one's relationship to it. The Sangha is the community. In its original use, the Sangha was the group of monks that formed one's community. In the West it is taken to be whatever spiritual community that one affiliates with. For example, it could be one's Buddhist friends, one's AA group, or one's church, synagogue or other religious fellowship. On a grand scale it could be thought of as one's connection to the entire family of man, or even beyond.

Buddhist understanding of Creation (see) differs from that of the West. The idea of God having created the world is so central to Judeo-Christian thinking that the first two stories in the Hebrew Bible are creation stories, two versions of the Adam and Eve in the Garden of Eden story. For Westerners, the idea that the world was not created by an all-powerful God is hard to grasp. Also challenging is the Buddhist idea of The Void, or Emptiness, an Eastern way of looking at creation. The Void is possibly most understandable in the concept of Ch'i, a Taoist belief. In Taoism, ch'i is the ground substance of existence, the breath of life. When ch'i consolidates, matter is formed, and eventually such matter dissolves back into ch'i. The origin of ch'i is not dealt with, as far as I understand, just as in Western religion the origin of God is not addressed. Here we have a remarkable similarity with the view of Albert Einstein who stated that matter is consolidation from the field, and that the field is the only reality. This agrees with the Buddhist idea of the non-permanence of things.

"In Buddhist teaching, 'emptiness' refers to a basic openness and nonseparation that we experience when all small and fixed notions of our self are seen through or dissolved. We experience it when we see that our existence is transitory, that our body, heart, and mind arise out of the changing web of life, where nothing is disconnected or separate."[154] We are all an aspect of the oneness of all things. As individuals we are properly viewed more as an aspect of the unity of all things rather than as an individual self with firm boundaries. "Emptiness (sunyata), from a Buddhist perspective, (is) an understanding of one's true nature, an intuition of the absence of inherent identity in people or things. It (is) the core psychological truth of Buddhism."[155] "Interbeing (is) the Buddhist teaching that nothing can be by itself alone, that everything in the cosmos must 'interbe' with everything else."[156]

Nirvana is the state of being extinguished, as in the blowing out of a candle. The end of suffering is contained in the third noble truth. Souls may wander through many lifetimes before achieving this understanding of no-self. Laura S. states that "what doesn't exist is a permanent, unchanging, separate, autonomous anything that can be called self."[157]

The Buddhist view of God's will is enlightenment for all beings. In this condition the universe will be at peace. The source of power to bring this about is love. The practices to bring this about are study, meditation, and the finding of a spiritual guide, a teacher. Through such practice the student comes to realize that his suffering is intimately connected with the suffering of all humanity. There is no real separation of individuals. The idea of an entirely distinct self is an illusion.

---

[154] Jack Kornfield, *A Path with Heart: A Guide through the Perils and Promises of Spiritual Life*, Bantam Books, 1993, 51.

[155] Mark Epstein, *Going to Pieces without Falling Apart: A Buddhist Perspective on Wholeness*, Harmony Books, 1998, 13.

[156] *Living Buddha, Living Christ*, 203.

[157] *12 Steps on Buddha's Path*, 13.

The Wisdom of Others

Thich Nhat Hanh

"Mindfulness is the key. When you become aware of something, you begin to have enlightenment… Mindfulness of breathing is your island, where you can be safe and happy…This is the way to take refuge in the Buddha, not as mere devotion but as a transformational practice…You can take refuge here and now. You only need to dwell deeply in the present moment." [158]

Jack Kornfield

"Strength of heart (MCG- Determination to pursue a spiritual path in life) comes from knowing that the pain that we each must bear is a part of the greater pain shared by all that lives….and realizing this awakens our universal compassion." [159]

MCG - Through the achievement of such understanding at an experiential level one arrives at the state of nirvana. This strikes me as a rather Christ-like concept, that is, taking on the suffering of others in love.

Kevin Griffin

"The Buddha says that recognizing our mistakes and admitting them is how we develop our spiritual life."[160] (MCG – AA steps, 4, 5, and 10)

"The St. Francis prayer, which appears in the chapter on Step Eleven of the book *Twelve Steps and Twelve Traditions,* points to the deepest truth

---

[158] *Living Buddha, Living Christ,* 116-117.
[159] *A Path with Heart,* 75.
[160] Kevin Griffin, *One Breath at a Time: Buddhism and the Twelve Steps,* Rodale 2004, 2017, 97.

about Non-Self when it says: 'For it is about self-forgetting that one finds… it is by dying that one awakens to Eternal Life.'" [161]

"The Buddha explains that any concept of I, me, or mine is inaccurate. Any time we try to nail down who we are, we miss something. We are a process: we are possibilities; and we constantly change."[162]

MCG - This again sounds like quantum physics (see). There are no actual definable, measurable particles, only probabilities of how such particles might interact.

"Insight into the three qualities of Impermanence, Suffering, and No-Self that Buddha said marked all existence—is the key to wisdom in the Buddhist tradition."[163]

[161] Ibid., 259.
[162] Ibid., 164.
[163] Ibid., 256.

Kabbalah

Kabbalah is a form of Jewish mysticism (see) whose origins can be found in the years after the destruction of the second temple in 70 CE. It became a more prominent movement in the thirteenth century, primarily in Spain. The principles of Kabbalah are to be found in the *Zohar* (*The Book of Splendor*) said to have been written by Rabbi Moses de Leon (1250-1305). Kabbalah appears to be a reaction to the rigid rabbinical interpretation of the Tanach (The Hebrew Bible, consisting of the five books of Moses, the books of the Prophets, and the Writings) found in the Talmud. The mystical system is far too complex to describe in detail here but suffice it to say that it represents a way of understanding God that goes beyond the black and white of the Bible. One might think of the words of the Bible as existing within a deeper consciousness, going beyond what can ultimately be represented by language or even thought. In Kabbalah, God is referred to as *Ein Sof,* meaning "without end." Another term referencing God is *Ayin*, meaning nothing, or no-thing. *Ayin* is also one of the two silent letters of the Hebrew alphabet. Neither of these names can be found in the Hebrew Bible.

According to the *Zohar,* God can be thought of as having a complex personality comprised of ten emanations from *Ayin*, known as *sefirot.* These emanations interact with each other in complex ways which will not be dealt with here, but the interested reader may do his or her own research. I caution that without a teacher one is more likely to become confused than illuminated by studying Kabbalah on one's own. (This is true of the pursuit of any spiritual path. It is always wise to have a spiritual advisor to help us stay on track on our spiritual path, whatever method we may be following. In AA that person is referred to as a sponsor, but the AA member may also find other people, such as a clergyman or a therapist, to supplement the sponsor's role.) In the Kabbalistic system each of the *sefirot* is associated with a body part and with a color. This is of interest, as within the Native American system (see) the four directions are also associated with colors. An element in this thought system is the importance of balance. The *sefirot* balance each other, and man plays a role in balancing the universe by acknowledging God and seeking to do His will. The *sefirot*, or components of God's personality, are:

Crown (*keter*) – This is God's thought at its deepest.

Wisdom (*chochmah*) - In this dimension God is starting to contemplate the creation of the world. So, before the existence of Torah there is said to be primordial Torah including a model of the universe in God's mind.

Understanding *(Binah)* – Here is God's completed conception of the form of the world. He has decided what form it is to take. An anthropomorphic understanding of *Binah* is that it is the highest of the feminine *sephirot*. It represents the womb wherein creation is impregnated by *Chochmah*. These first three sefirot describe the thought process and contents of God. (Einstein (see) also talked about how God thinks, saying that God's thoughts are reflected in the laws of nature.)

Compassion (*Chesed*) - Also known as lovingkindness.

Judgment *(Gevurah)* - Also sometimes translated as might. This is the aspect of God as angry and punitive that we find in places in the Hebrew Bible.

Beauty *(Tiferet)* – Also thought of as glory.

Victory *(Netzah)*

Splendor *(Hod)*

Foundation *(Yesod)*

Sovereignty *(Malchut)*

Here are several names for God encompassed within Kabbalistic thought. Some are specifically associated with one of the *sephirot*. (See also Appendix B – Names of God.)

Ehyeh – Associated with *Keter* – This name is found in the Torah. God has instructed Moses to go to the Pharaoh and demand that the Hebrew people be allowed to leave Egypt, and Moses asked God "who shall I say sent me?" God replied "*Ehyeh asher ehyeh*" – "I will be what I will be"; or "I am that I am."

Shechinah – The Divine Presence. Associated with *Malkhut*. This is a feminine word, and references God as a spiritual presence. As such, it approximates God as the Holy Spirit in Christianity or the Great Spirit in Native American spirituality.

Elohim – Associated with *Binah* and also with *Gevurah*. It is a plural form of the name *El*.

Adonai Tzvaot – Lord of Hosts – Associated with *Netzah*. In the Bible the hosts seem to refer to the multitude of angels.

Elohim Tzvaot – God of Hosts – Associated with *Hod*

El Hai – The Living God – Associated with *Yesod*.

El Shaddai – God Almighty – Also associated with *Yesod*.

One can find diagrams that show how these sephirot relate to each other in complex ways. Often the diagram is in a human form in which various *sephirot* are associated with certain areas of the body.

Some fascinating things can be found in Kabbalistic writing, including a description of what corresponds to the Big Bang theory, by Moses de Leon. "The beginning of existence is the secret concealed point. The is the beginning of all the hidden things, which spread out from there and emanate, according to their species. From a single point you can extend the dimensions of all things; similarly, when the concealed arouses itself to exist, at first it brings into being something the size of the point of a needle; from there it generates everything."[164]

---

[164] Daniel C. Matt, *God and the Big Bang: Discovering Harmony between Science & Spirituality*, Jewish Lights Publishing, 1996, 2016, 25.

There is an understanding in Kabbalah that nothing is separate from God. Another important thought is that God requires man for God to be realized. It is as though God cannot exist until man tries to approach Him with understanding and love. It is understood that God will meet man more than halfway in this attempt to unite.

The Wisdom of Others

Daniel C. Matt

"The name *Ein Sof* opens with a negative, *Ein,* 'there is no.' This accords with the view of the philosopher Moses Maimonides that it is more accurate to say what God is not than what God is."[165]

"Another kabbalistic name for God is *Ayin,* 'nothingness.' It conveys the idea that God is no thing: God animates all things and cannot be contained by any of them."[166]

He quotes Meister Eckhart: "God's nothingness fills the entire world; his something though is nowhere."[167]

MCG – Here is a stunning use of paradox.

"Material existence emerges out of *Ayin,* 'no-thingness,' the divine pool of energy. Ultimately, the world is not other than God, for this energy is concealed within all forms of being."[168]

MCG – Here again, as in Native American spirituality, we find the concept of panentheism.

"By contemplating the *sefirot,* one explores the emotional and psychological texture of God's various personal qualities, such as love,

---

[165] Ibid., 23.
[166] Ibid., 24.
[167] Ibid., 24.
[168] Ibid., 29.

fear, and compassion…. The *sefirot* are tools for meditation. Each serves as a focus for visualization, disclosing depths of archetypal personality within God and the seeker."[169]

"We need God to remind us that we are part of God, since we constantly forget. And God needs us to mend the fractured world. In Kabbalah, God's need is called 'the need on high.' And without us, God is incomplete: The divine sparks remain hidden, the divine potential is unrealized. By mending the world—socially, economically, politically—we mend God and mend what is torn within us, between us, and around us."[170]

Adin Steinsaltz

"The human soul, from its lowest to its highest levels, is a unique and single entity, even though it is many-faceted. In its profoundest being, the soul of man is part of the Divine and, in this respect, is a manifestation of God in the world."[171]

"Every person has his own spiritual essence whose uniqueness not only is the result of his heredity and education but exists by divine intention. For each and every human being has a specific task to perform in the world, a task that no one else can accomplish, though there well may be better and more gifted people around to do it. "[172]

"When a man learns that just as he broods over himself so does God yearn for him and look for him, he is at the beginning of a higher level of consciousness…. For in truth, it is not one question with two sides but a meeting place of two questions, that of man seeking himself and of God seeking man. Together they can approach a solution of the problem of man's existence."[173]

---

[169] Ibid., 38.
[170] Ibid., 137.
[171] *The Thirteen Petalled Rose*, 51.
[172] Ibid., 101-102.
[173] Ibid., 148.

Albert Einstein

It is worthwhile, in our search for a higher power, to examine the ideas of Albert Einstein on ethics, morality, and religion. As a renowned genius, his thoughts about a higher power deserve to be considered. As a child he grew up in a Jewish home, but religion as such was not practiced in the home. When he was 4 or 5 years old his father gave him a compass. This device fascinated him, and for the first time it occurred to him that things are not as straightforward as they might seem, that there are forces deeply hidden in the world. This sense of wonder stimulated his curiosity, and he spent his lifetime attempting to answer such questions as the nature of matter, of time, and how things might relate to each other. The mystery (see) appealed to him and stimulated him. He viewed mystery as beautiful, the source of and inspiration for both art and science. His mind was highly developed in the sense that he had a great comprehension of mathematics and was able to use it in his contemplation of problems in physics. He had a remarkable capacity to concentrate, to hold a thought in his mind as he examined multiple aspects of a problem. According to physicist Sabine Hossenfelder, no computer has yet been able to use all its store of data to fully develop Einstein's theories of relativity. Einstein realized that to get at the truth, before formulating an answer to a problem, one had to know exactly what question to ask. Still, he realized that knowledge was not an ultimate goal. He was fond of saying that imagination is more important than knowledge because it has no limits. It occurs to me that imagination may be more helpful to get closer to an understanding about a higher power than knowledge. Einstein's contribution to our understanding of the physical world placed him substantially above others whose genius is also unquestionable. In fact, in 1999 he was named the Person of the Century by Time magazine for his contributions to scientific progress.

In terms of the relationship of people to each other, he was opposed to war and other violent solutions to human disagreement. Although a pacifist, he found it necessary to warn President Roosevelt of the fact that Germany was working on an atomic bomb, and that America needed to take steps to secure a supply of uranium ore, and to develop such a bomb before the Germans had one. He was a believer in the importance of the Golden Rule, of service to others rather than pursuing a life of self-aggrandizement. He was a modest man, humble and grateful for what gifts he was given in life. As did Bill Wilson, Einstein believed that the measure of success in a person's life depends upon his development of humility and upon pursuit of goals that benefit others.

Einstein realized that at some level truth will remain elusive, that one discovery will lead to more questions that defy easy resolution. He insisted that proofs of theories be based on reproduceable experiments leading to solid evidence. For this reason, he never could accept quantum mechanics which relies on stating probabilities (for example, of where particles might be and how they relate to each other at any given time) rather than an actual measurement. His statement about the quantum theory was "God does not play with dice."[174]

Along the same lines of dealing with trying to determine the truth, he was fond of saying "As far as the laws of mathematics refer to reality, they are not certain; and as far as they are certain, they do not refer to reality." (This supports the comment of my daughter who was extremely frustrated with high school mathematics and proclaimed that "math is bull****." But of course, it is not bull****, but it is merely incomprehensible to many of us mortals.) He was also fond of saying "Science without religion is lame; religion without science is blind." He also was known to say, "What I see convinces me that God exists; what I cannot see confirms it." This underscores his belief that the physical world is far from the only reality. In fact, his thinking was similar to Eastern thought. The mystics of the East saw all physical manifestations as transitory and illusory.

---

[174] Jeremy Bernstein, *Einstein*, Viking Press, 1973, 192.

He spoke at times about his thoughts about God and religion. While he did not believe in a conventional Western conception of God, he insisted that he was not an atheist. A term he sometimes used for God is "The Old One." He used to say that he agreed with Spinoza about God. Spinoza was a rationalist who did not believe that God put us here to test or judge us. Heaven and hell (see) are states that we create for ourselves here on earth in this life. Einstein did not believe that people can have a personal relationship with a higher power, nor did he believe in life after death, at least not in the sense that one's spiritual self remains intact and distinct from all others. His idea of God had to do with the intelligent order found within the universe, and upon which the universe exists. This agrees with the approach taken by some in AA who think of God in terms of "Good Orderly Direction." Religion was mostly a matter of ethics for Einstein, although he said that being Jewish was important to him, and became more so as he got older.

Einstein believed that we are here on earth for a purpose. That purpose is to be of benefit to others. We are to understand that what we are and what we have, we owe to others. His ideals were beauty, goodness, and truth. Among the most wonderful things is the mysterious, the source of art and science. He did not believe that there is a God who metes out rewards and punishments, nor that the personhood survives the death of the body. However, he did think that there is a consciousness in the universe that is eternal in nature in which we all participate.

Quantum Physics

The study of quantum physics can be of value in the search for a higher power. I wish I could write a more coherent rational explanation of how and why this is so. While in some respects my mind is very good, there are other areas of significant limitation in my ability to grasp concepts. Nowhere am I weaker than with mathematics. Therefore, theoretical physics is beyond my reach. Nevertheless, I will do my best, supported by the thoughts of others.

Why should we be interested in quantum physics, especially given the likelihood that we may not understand it very well? There are two reasons I believe it is worthwhile to think about this. One is the field of quantum physics offers us the principle of uncertainty which tells us that we cannot say much that is certain about the physical world, especially at the level of subatomic particles. Uncertainty also extends to the topic under consideration here—the higher power. Secondly and more importantly from my point of view, we have the remarkable fact that as one digs deeper into quantum theory, one arrives at a similar understanding of the universe (and thus, a higher power) that have been found by the masters of Eastern philosophy.

From the standpoint of subatomic physics, as Fritjof Capra wrote, "Quantum theory has thus demolished the classical concepts of solid objects and of strictly deterministic laws of nature. At the subatomic level, the solid material objects of classical physics dissolve into wave-like patterns of probabilities, and these patterns, ultimately, do not represent probabilities of things, but rather probabilities of interconnections. A careful analysis of the process of observation in atomic physics has shown that the subatomic particles have no meaning as isolated entities, but rather probabilities of interconnections between the preparation of an experiment and the subsequent measurement. Quantum theory thus reveals a basic oneness of the universe. It shows that we cannot decompose the world into independently existing smallest units."[175]

WHAT??? This goes completely against what I thought that I understood about the physical world. I always assumed that if your microscope was strong enough, you could observe the basic building blocks of the universe. But if I understand the above statements correctly, insofar as they are true, there are no basic building blocks of the universe. Rather, there are probabilities of where these subatomic particles might be, if they exist, and more importantly, how they relate to each other. While quantum theory remains a theory it has held up over the past one hundred years of scientific scrutiny and testing. Other proposals have been offered to explain the nature of matter, such as string theory, but nothing has convinced most physicists to abandon quantum theory. It is noteworthy that Einstein was one who never bought into quantum theory, saying famously that "God does not play with dice."

Capra pointed out the remarkable similarity between quantum theory and Eastern mysticism. "The Eastern sages make it clear that they do not mean ordinary emptiness when they talk about Brahman, sunyata, or Tao, but on the contrary, a Void which has an infinite creative potential. Thus, the Void of the Eastern mystics can easily be compared to the quantum field of subatomic physics. Like the quantum field, it gives birth to an infinite variety of forms which it sustains and, eventually, reabsorbs....

"The Neo-Confucians developed a notion of ch'i which bears the most striking resemblance to the concept of the quantum field in modern physics. Like the quantum field, ch'i is conceived as a tenuous and non-perceptible form of matter which is present throughout space and can condense into solid material objects"[176] "Thus ch'i condenses and disperses rhythmically, bringing forth all forms which eventually dissolve into the

---

[175] *The Tao of Physics,* 69.
[176] Ibid., 213.

Void…As Chang Tsai says: 'The Great Void cannot but consist of ch'i; this ch'i cannot but condense to form all things; and these things cannot but become dispersed so as to form (once more) the Great Void.'" [177]

It is remarkable that such similar ideas arose in such different systems of thought. While I don't expect my readers to become Eastern mystics or nuclear physicists, I believe that it is worthwhile to at least consider these ideas for a moment. Why? Because we are searching, seeking a higher power. If there is another path to follow, to investigate, we should take advantage and see what we can find.

---

[177] Ibid., 214.

Conclusion

Higher power is a tough topic for most people, especially people who want a solid foundation to stand on. I believe that people who already have a clear idea of their own higher power would have had no need to read this book, so I address these comments to the uncertain majority. I put many ideas and suggestions to think about together and left a lot out as well. I didn't want the book to be burdensome. To write a comprehensive book about all ideas about a higher power would be encyclopedic in scope. Many other resources are available including those listed in both my bibliography and my suggested reading list. The search for a higher power has been a journey for me, and it is ongoing. My suggestion of seeking a higher power that you like and makes you feel loved, or at least feel good, is a positive approach that should be fruitful. Whether your interest began in addiction or family recovery or in relation to some other challenging circumstance in your life, I hope you have picked up something of value somewhere in these pages. I do wish you much happiness, safe travels, and satisfaction in your life.

Appendix A

The God Word in Alcoholics Anonymous Literature

Many people who have never been to an AA meeting have an idea that it is a religious organization of some kind. About half of such people who could potentially benefit from affiliating with AA are reluctant to do so because they don't want to be preached to or to hear about God. While AA in fact is not a religious denomination at all, these prejudices can easily be reinforced by attendance at a meeting, especially if the various speakers talk about what God has done for them, and by observing the slogans and twelve steps hanging on the wall, liberally mentioning God. Most people, once at a meeting, feel relatively positive about the group, and are often advised to "not worry about the God stuff," and to just "keep coming back." For many this works out well, but not for everybody.

AA developed a formula of referring to a higher power, saying, "God as you understand him." It goes back to the origins of the program when Ebby T., the man who brought the idea to Bill Wilson, suggested that Bill use his own conception of God. Despite efforts to open the door wide for everyone to cross the threshold, there remains a lot of "God" in the program, regrettably, too much for some people.

I have gone through the fourth edition of *Alcoholics Anonymous*, just the forwards though page 164 where the basic explanation of the program concludes. The remainer of the book is mostly stories of members, telling what their life had been like, what happened to change it, and what it is like now. I inventoried all the "God" references. This is what I found, and of course, what anyone else would find if they read the book.

References to a divine being, followed by the number of times one finds it:

God – 136

He/Him/His/Himself – 54

God as we/you understood Him – 3

Creator – 10

Creative Intelligence – 1

All-Powerful Guiding Creative Intelligence - 1

Universal Mind - 1

Spirit of the Universe – 4

Sunlight of the Spirit – 1

Fellowship of the Spirit – 1

His Spirit – 1

Realm of the Spirit – 1

Spirit of Nature – 1

Supreme Being – 2

Czar of the Heavens – 1

Great Reality – 1

Father of Light – 1

Christ – 1

My new-found Friend – 1

Director – 1

Principal - 1

Father – 1

Employer – 1

Maker – 1

Thee/Thy/Thou – 10

Power references

Power greater than ourselves/himself – 9

higher power – 2

Power – 3

Presence and Power of God – 1

Presence of Infinite Power and Love - 1

Loving and All-Powerful Creator – 1

This book was published in 1939 when the fellowship was barely four years old. Almost ten years later a follow-up text, *Twelve Steps and Twelve Traditions,* was published, also authored by Bill Wilson. By this time AA was very well-established, and if there was any motivation to downplay the "God stuff" the book would have reflected this. Here is my inventory of "God words" in *Twelve Steps and Twelve Traditions.*

References to a divine being, followed by the number of times one finds it:

God – 162

God as you understand Him – 6

higher power – 18

Power greater than ourselves – 5

Him/His/He/Himself – 40

Creator – 5

Lord – 1

Master – 1

Father – 1

The Hand of Providence – 1

Thy – 3

Several things are notable. First, Bill has not backed off from the God word. By the way, I am not suggesting that he should have, I am only observing that AA has every appearance of presenting itself as a God-based program. Next, the references to "God as you understand him" are few and far between, three in *Alcoholic Anonymous,* and six in *Twelve Steps and Twelve Traditions.* However, the number of references to a "higher power" increased considerably from the first to the second book. There are two in *Alcoholics Anonymous* and eighteen in *Twelve Steps and Twelve Traditions.* This suggests that Wilson was getting more comfortable with this terminology, and it suggests that this would be true within the program as well. Indeed, Wilson suggests from the beginning that a person needs to find a power greater than himself to be "restored to sanity." He does not insist that this higher power be God, although he does talk about God a lot. Another notable thing is that in the second book Bill dropped much of the fancy New Thought terminology used in the first book. We are not treated to the "sunlight of the spirit" in his second book.

I included this appendix only to make a point— that there is a lot of the God word in *Alcoholics Anonymous*. It is partly for this reason that I wrote this book. I wanted to present ideas to people who are trying to find a way to be comfortable in the AA program, and to find it an effective means of recovery from a devastating addiction, without having to think specifically about God. And I wanted to suggest what could be new or different ways of thinking about God that could make more sense or be more acceptable to some people who are, indeed, searching. To be fair, my book suffers (if that is the right word) from the same frequent mentioning of God as that of the two principal AA texts. I suspect that I may have talked too much about God. The fact is that I have used the God word more often than did Bill Wilson. Here is the inventory of God words in my Second Step guide. I have surveyed the main text of the book, but did not include the appendices. The word "God" appears 366 times in this book, so I obviously didn't avoid it. This is more than double that of either the books *Alcoholics Anonymous* or *Twelve Steps and Twelve Traditions*. So, if I was trying to avoid the God word I certainly did not succeed. To be fair, of the 366 times the word "God" appears in the text, 86 of those times it was when I was quoting others. So, maybe we can say the I used the word "God" in my own writing just 280 times—still, a lot. On the other hand, not counting the appendices, the phrase "higher power" appears 262 times, making me believe that I did make a substantial shift towards the idea of a higher power. (You will recall, as noted above, that the phrase "higher power" appeared twice in the Big Book and 18 times in *Twelve Steps and Twelve Traditions*.)

Appendix B
Names of God

It is possible that readers may be inspired in the search for a higher power by discovering a name of God that makes sense to them. For this reason, I include this section on names of God.

Father Ed Dowling, Bill Wilson's spiritual advisor used to say that once you give God a name you have missed the boat. Any name imposes an artificial limit. The presentation here is just to give some direction. It is like pointing one's finger at the moon. The finger doesn't give much of an idea about the moon other than suggesting where to look. I include here just a few of the thousands of names that point at the higher power.

Native American names

In *Rainbow Tribe,* author Ed McGaa suggests the term Great Mystery to refer to the higher power, not to be specifically accurate, but to "leave adequate latitude and to avoid an argument."[178]

He says the expression Gitchi-Manitou is the Ojibwa's way of saying the Great Spirit or the Great Mystery.[179]

---

[178] Ed McGaa, Eagle Man, *Rainbow Tribe, 4.*
[179] Ibid., 200.

Here are some other Indigenous American names for the higher power:

Kche Mnedo: "Great Spirit" – Potawatomi
Mamogosnan – Creator - Potowatomi[180]
Wakan Tanka – Great Spirit or Great Mystery – Oglala Sioux[181]

Lame Deer Seeker of Visions by John (Fire) Lame Deer and Richard Erdoes

"The force which animates all things in the universe is called *Takuskanska*, ('that which moves') the moving spirit, the energy of natural processes."

"The old word for god and the old word for stone are the same—*tunkashila*, grandfather—but it is also a name for the Great Spirit."[182]

Terms from Islam

In his book, *99 Names of God,* Brother David Steindl-Rast, expounds upon some of the ideas behind trying to name God, describing certain aspects of personality that are imagined as attributable to God. In this book he delves into the Muslim tradition. I have selected twenty-one of these names along with some of Brother David's commentary.

"al-Malik – The KING

"It is doubly dangerous to call God KING. First, it may suggest ascribing to God qualities that often characterize worldly kings. This would be a serious mistake. Kings boast, whereas God's workings are hidden. Kings oppress; God empowers. Kings enforce obedience; God gives the gift of freedom."[183]

---

[180] http://www.native-languages.org › potawatomi-legends.
[181] *Mother Earth Spirituality,* 214.
[182] Ibid., 193.
[183] Brother David Steindl-Rast, *99 Names of God,* Orbis Books, 2021, 14.

"*as-Salaam* – the PEACE – The Giver of Peace

"PEACE…. Is the dynamic stillness of a calmly burning candle flame and is rooted in an all-encompassing order, the ordering principle of which is love: love as a lived Yes to the mutual belonging of all to all." [184]

"*al-Muhayim* – the GUARDIAN and keeper

"Desperation makes us blind to the possibilities that, despite everything, are still open to us. Trust, however, opens our eyes and lets us discover unexpected paths forward. In this, God reveals himself as the GUARDIAN. He works on us not 'from the outside in,' but from the innermost depth of the Mystery in which our life is rooted."[185]

"*al-Azeez* – the ALMIGHTY, the Venerable

"Again and again, people show their love of power. But with God, it is about the power of love. Only love deserves to be called almighty. Why? Because there is nothing—truly, absolutely nothing—that love cannot transform and turn to good. Power, then, is not simply an attribute of God the ALMIGHTY. Rather, God is almightiness because God is love."[186]

MCG - So, looking at it in this way, love is the highest power in the universe.

"al-*Jabbar* – the POWERFUL

"Is our own power of life not itself an experience of that 'higher power'? And the more science learns about how things 'work,' the more mysterious we find the origins and nature of the power of life. In the end, by calling God the POWERFUL, we are not ascribing to him some trait. Instead,

---

[184] Ibid., 18.
[185] Ibid., 22-23.
[186] Ibid., 24-25.

we are reverentially pointing to that 'higher power' that acts within us and yet remains forever unfathomable."[187]

"al-Mutakabbir – the TRANSCENDENT,
the Supreme, the Majestic."[188]

"al-Khaaliq – the CREATOR

"God does not work on the world 'from outside.' Instead, the name CREATOR points to the magnitude of the Mystery from whose creative power all that is given proceeds."[189]

"al-Baari – the ORIGIN

"We can work creatively only with what has already been created, with what is already there. But how is it that there is anything at all, rather than nothing? Etymologically, the word 'ORIGIN' comes from the image of rising or leaping forth...Being leaps into existence from non-being."[190]

"al-'Aleem – the ALL-COMPREHENDING, the All-Knowing[191]

"as-Samee' – the ALL-HEARING ONE.

"God's names—which we should perhaps think of as clues to God—point to an Ultimate Reality that is forever inexpressible... Those names say something not only about us, but about God, as well. The little ladybug that lands on my finger has a true experience of me, however limited that

---

[187] Ibid., 26-27.
[188] Ibid., 28.
[189] Ibid., 30.
[190] Ibid., 32.
[191] Ibid., 46.

experience may be. If it could be put into words, the ladybug would say something about me that is true."[192]

"al-'Azeem – the SUBLIME, the Supreme, the Magnificent

"The meaning of sublimity and magnificence is brought home to us in those moments psychology refers to as peak experiences… But the sublimity we become conscious of during peak experiences is infinitely beyond anything our senses can fully grasp."[193]

He quotes a teacher he called wise: "God is not watching over your every step in order to catch you out in every mistake. No! God loves you so much that he can't take his eyes off you."[194]

"al-Waasi' – the ALL-ENCOMPASSING, the Boundless

"The Ultimate Reality can exclude nothing… This naming involves far more than a logical conclusion. Such a divine name could only come from a mystical insight, which goes beyond logic but without contradicting it. The ALL-ENCOMPASSING must, for example, encompass Non-being as well as Being."[195]

"al-Wadood – the ALL-LOVING

"Any being—anything that is—becomes what it is only through its relationship to other things that are, and comes to belong to itself only through love, through this Yes. Anything we say about love resonates with all the joy and fulness of life we know from our human, loving relationships.[196]

---

[192] Ibid., 60.
[193] Ibid., 74.
[194] Ibid., 95.
[195] Ibid., 98.
[196] Ibid., 102-103.

"al-Haqq – the ABSOLUTE TRUTH

"At issue is not one particular truth or another, but truth in and of itself. As soon as we express an insight into truth, it becomes only a partial truth, for words and concepts can never grasp the entirety of truth. But the human heart longs for all-encompassing truth, and we can sense such truth only beyond words and concepts. The word 'God' points to an undoubtable reality—just like the word 'There' in the sentence, 'There is a universe.'"[197]

"al-Wakeel – the TRUSTWORTHY, the dependable
Helper and Guardian, the Trustee

"When we speak this name, we are emphasizing that we trust God. At the same time, the name points to a significant distinction: the distinction between believing something, in the sense of considering something true, and belief in something, in the sense of trusting. When I believe something, then in the end I am trusting myself... But when I believe in someone, then I am relying on that person. What a radical statement! It means that I leave the realm of my own reasoned discernment and enter into a highly personal relationship of trust.[198]

"In all these divine names, it is not so much about fixed idea of God, but about relationship: the relationship between my 'I' and the divine 'Thou.'"[199]

MCG – This sounds like Martin Buber who wrote extensively about the "I-Thou relationship".

---

[197] Ibid., 110.
[198] Ibid., 112.
[199] Ibid., 114.

"al-Mubdi' – the ALL-BEGINNING, the Initiator

"At a certain age, children often ask tirelessly where things come from. When we began to think, we were all little philosophers, driven to philosophical questioning by one thing: wonderment. Plato knew that philosophy begins with wonderment, and as children, we were still capable of wondering at the fact that there exists something rather than nothing."[200]

"al-Qayyoom – the ETERNAL

"Eternity remains; time runs out... We are also familiar with the Now as the intersection of time and eternity. And we know, because in the Now we take part in a truth that is not subject to time, that our existence transcends time... We experience time as growth and decay, but the Now as fulfilled reality. I can't stop my decay in time, but I can counter it with Self-fulfillment in the Now. Every spiritual practice aims to serve this purpose by leading to the Now and to an encounter with the ETERNAL."[201]

"al-Waajid – the GIVER OF BEING

"When we name that Ultimate Reality to which we as human beings are oriented, two things occur: we become consciously aware of a Higher Power in our lives, and we open ourselves up to a personal relationship with that power by addressing it by name."[202]

"al-Awwal – the FIRST WITHOUT BEGINNING."[203]

"al-Aakhir – the LAST WITHOUT END."[204]

---

[200] Ibid., 124.
[201] Ibid., 134-135.
[202] Ibid., 136.
[203] Ibid., 154.
[204] Ibid., 156.

"an-Nur – the LIGHT."[205]

MCG - Contrasting with these lofty ideas is the expression "the man upstairs" which seems to satisfy many people.

Here are three thoughts from Mel Ash.

"Concerning the Tao, Lao-tzu in *Tao te Ching*, or '*Classic of the Way of Power*,' said, 'Tao can be spoken about, but not the eternal, unchanging Tao. Things can be named, but not the ultimate name.'"[206]

"Call it God, call it Zen, call it anything you like, but just don't call it Too Late to save yourself from yourself."[207]

"I don't call my higher power anything at all. My collection of bargain-basement bodhisattvas and Salvation Army saviors reminds me that if I do so, I'm already dead and defined, unable to flow with the ever-changing and ever-passing world. The God that can be named is not God."[208]

Here are some of the hundreds of names found in the Jewish tradition:

HaRachaman – The Compassionate one

Ribon HaOlam – Master of the Universe

HaShem – The Name. Because the second of the Ten Commandments says to not take God's name in vain, traditional Jewish observance often restricts the reference to God as "The Name", or *HaShem*. And the word God is often rendered G-d in print. However, in the context of the liturgy in a worship service God's name may be used.

Adonai - Lord

---

[205] Ibid., 194.
[206] *The Zen of Recovery*, 42.
[207] Ibid., 181.
[208] Ibid., 215.

El Elyon – God on High

Elohim - God

Ein Sof – Without end – A traditional name seen in Kabbala (See).

Adonai tzvaot - Lord of hosts

Elohim tzvoat – God of hosts

El Hai – The living God

Shechinah – The Spirit

El Shaddai – God almighty

Ehyeh – I am, or I will be

The Holy One, Blessed be He

God of Abraham, God of Isaac, and God of Jacob

God of Sarah, God of Rebecca, God of Rachel, and God of Leah

Jehovah, Yahweh – The name suggested by the Tetragrammaton, YHVH

Matthew Fox

"The *Tao Te Ching* calls God 'the Great Mother of the Universe.'"[209]

The *Bhagavad Gita*: "God has a million faces."[210]

"The ancient Vedas of India tell us that "The One Existence the wise call by many names."[211]

---

[209] *Naming the Unnamable*, 73.
[210] Ibid., xxv.
[211] Ibid., xxiii.

"As Augustine put it, 'If you comprehend it, it is not God.'"[212]

"Deepak Chopra calls God the 'self of the universe.'"[213]

Other names from *The Divine Within* by Aldous Huxley, Preface by Jacqueline Hazard Bridgeman.[214]

The Divine Ground of our Being

The Fat Lady – J. D. Salinger

The Force – George Lucas in *Star Wars*

The Divine Spark – Emerson

higher power – Bill Wilson in *Alcoholics Anonymous*

GOD acronyms often heard in Alcoholics Anonymous circles:

Good Orderly Direction

Group Of Drunks

Gift Of Desperation

Great Out-Doors

[212] Ibid., xxxi.
[213] Ibid.,18.
[214] Aldous Huxley, *The Divine Within, Preface by Jacqueline Hazard Bridgeman,* HarperPerennial Modern Classics, 1992, (Preface), ix.

Appendix C

It's the Truth

I don't know if this is true or not, but Confucius supposedly once said, "Last night I dreamed that I was a butterfly. How do I know that I am not a butterfly dreaming that I am a person?" How, indeed? How can I be sure that I am right about anything? If everyone in a room full of people agrees on a certain fact, say, that today is Sunday (as I am writing this, it is Sunday according to today's newspaper), does this establish that today is Sunday? If anything can be certain about this, it is that everyone has agreed that it is Sunday. That it is Sunday is not certain. I have written earlier about Professor Einstein who had certain ideas about the relativity of time, which admittedly I do not understand. What I do believe is that almost nothing is certain. Not even mathematics. Einstein said this about math. "As far as the laws of mathematics refer to reality, they are not certain; and as far as they are certain, they do not refer to reality." If this is true, then what can we rely on? Does one plus one equal two, or doesn't it?

I am making an issue out of this for a reason. As one searches for a higher power, he or she will encounter a great variety of evidence and opinion. Some people will state a certain "fact" with absolute assurance that they are right. Being passionate about what one believes does not make them right. Or, at least, it may be that what they are right about applies only to them— not necessarily to anyone else. If you choose to believe anything that I claim to be true, I hope that it is this: Truth is relative. What is true for me may or may not be true for you. Professor Heisenberg proposed the Uncertainty Principle that expresses the "fact" that there is a limit to what we can know about subatomic physics. As I wrote in my essay on quantum physics, it is impossible to measure everything of that degree of smallness simultaneously. What we are left with are probabilities of associations between particles. Or maybe there are no particles. Maybe the existence of the ultimate building blocks of matter is a myth.

How are we to conduct a search for a higher power if there is no certainty about anything, especially anything as important as the existence of or identity of a higher power? I believe that we all have our own truth, and that if we are honest, open-minded, and motivated to find our truth, what we find will be true enough for us. We can't just throw up our hands and say, "It is hopeless." We have been advised that to recover from our addiction we must rely on a power greater than ourselves. While this may not be true, it is wise to proceed as though it is because of our past failures to overcome our addiction unaided. It is likely that as one progresses in this search, certain things will make sense and add up to a working understanding and acceptance of an effective higher power. This is all you need. And if, over time, certain other things come into focus, and your understanding changes, this is simply an expected part of the process. If other people have a different understanding that works for them, why is that a problem? We need to be honest in our search, and respectful of others in our community of recovering people who are searching in their own way. And remember, (your) truth will set you free.

Appendix D

The Twelve Steps of Alcoholics Anonymous

1) We admitted that we were powerless over alcohol—that our lives had become unmanageable.

2) Came to believe that a power greater than ourselves could restore us to sanity.

3) Made a decision to turn our will and our lives over to the care of God *as we understood Him*.

4) Made a searching and fearless moral inventory of ourselves.

5) Admitted to God, to ourselves, and to another human being the exact nature of our wrongs.

6) Were entirely ready to have God remove all these defects of character.

7) Humbly asked Him to remove our shortcomings.

8) Made a list of all persons we had harmed, and became willing to make amends to them all.

9) Made direct amends to such people wherever possible, except when to do so would injure them or others.

10) Continued to take personal inventory and when we were wrong promptly admitted it.

11) Sought through prayer and meditation to improve our conscious contact with God *as we understood Him*, praying only for the knowledge of His will for us and the power to carry that out.

12) Having had a spiritual awakening as the result of these steps, we tried to carry this message to alcoholics, and to practice these principles in all our affairs.[215]

---

[215] *Alcoholics Anonymous*, 59-60.

Bibliography

Ackroyd, Eric. *A Dictionary of Dream Symbols (With an Introduction to Dream Psychology)*. Blandford, 1993.

Alcoholics Anonymous: The Story of How Many Thousands of Men and Women Have Recovered from Alcoholism. Alcoholics Anonymous World Services, Inc. 4th ed., 2001.

Alexander, William. *Ordinary Recovery: Mindfulness, Addiction, and the Path of Lifelong Sobriety.* Shambala, 2010.

Allen, Mike. Axios Daily News Feed. Presented by United for Democracy, March 29, 2024.

American Family Survey, Deseret News. December 6, 2017.

Ash, Mel. *The Zen of Recovery.* Jeremy P. Tarcher/Putnam, 1993.

Bernstein, Jeremy. *Einstein.* Viking Press, Inc., 1973.

Bidwell, Duane R. *When One Religion Isn't Enough: The Lives of Spiritually Fluid People.* Beacon Press, 2018.

Black Elk with Neihardt, John G. *Black Elk Speaks: Being the Life Story of a Holy Man of the Oglala Sioux.* University of Nebraska Press, 1932, 1959, 1961, 1972.

Bridgeman, Jacqueline Hazard in Huxley, Aldous. *The Divine Within, Preface.* HarperPerennial Modern Classics, 1992.

Brown, Joseph Epes. *The Sacred Pipe: Black Elk's Account of the Seven Rites of the Oglala Sioux.* University of Oklahoma Press, 1953, 1989.

Buber, Martin. *Hasidism and Modern Man*. Humanities Press International, Inc., 1958, 1988.

Came to Believe: The Spiritual Adventure of AA as Experienced by Individual Members. Alcoholics Anonymous World Services, Inc. 1973, From a Grapevine article by Bill Wilson, April 1961.

Campbell, Joseph. *The Hero with a Thousand Faces*. Princeton University Press, 1949.

Campbell, Joseph with Bill Moyers. *The Power of Myth*. Anchor Books, 1988, 1991.

Capra, Fritjof. *The Tao of Physics: An Exploration of the Parallels between Modern Physics and Eastern Mysticism*. Shambala, 2010.

C. Chuck. *A New Pair of Glasses*. New-Look Publishing Company, 1984.

Deloria, Vine, Jr. *God Is Red: A Native View of Religion*. Fulcrum Publishing, 1973, 1992, 2003, 2023.

Dr. Bob and the Good Oldtimers. Alcoholics Anonymous World Services, Inc., 1980.

Epstein, Mark. *Going to Pieces without Falling Apart: A Buddhist Perspective on Wholeness*. Harmony Books, 1998.

F. Andy. *The Twelve Steps for Agnostics*.

Fox, Emmet. *The Sermon on the Mount*. HarperSanFrancisco, 1934, 1935, 1938.

Fox, Matthew. *Naming the Unnamable: 89 Wonderful and Useful Names for God...Including the Unnamable God*. Little Bound Books, 2018.

Fox, Matthew. *Meister Eckhart: A Mystic-Warrior for Our Times*. New World Library, Novato, CA, www.newworldlibrary.com, 2014.

Fromm, Erich. *The Art of Loving*. Harper & Brothers Publishers, 1956.

Gordon, Michael Cowl. *The Twelve Step Pathway: A Heroic Journey of Recovery*. Rowman & Littlefield, 2023.

Grapevine Word for the Day, April 20, 2024. *From Make Believe to Belief*. Charleston, West Virginia, June 1981, *Voices of Long-Term Sobriety*.

Griffin, Kevin. *One Breath at a Time: Buddhism and the Twelve Steps*. Rodale, 2004, 2017.

Gros, Frederic. *A Philosophy of Walking*. First edition translated by John Howe 2014, 2015, 2023; Translation of chapters 12, 15, 18, 21, 23, 24, 33 by Andy Bliss 2023. Verso, 2014, 2023. First published in German as *Marcher, une philosophie*. Flammarion, 2011.

Hanh, Thich Nhat. *Living Buddha, Living Christ*. Riverhead Books, 1995.

Heschel, Abraham Joshua. *God in Search of Man: A Philosophy of Judaism*. Farrar, Straus, and Giroux, 1955.

Heschel, Abraham Joshua. *I Asked for Wonder*, edited by Samual Dresler. Crossroad, 1993.

Heschel, Abraham Joshua. *Man Is not Alone: A Philosophy of Religion*. Farrar, Straus, and Giroux, 1951.

Heschel, Abraham Joshua. *Man's Quest for God: Studies in Prayer and Symbolism*. Charles Scribner's Sons, 1954.

Heschel, Abraham Joshua. *The Insecurity of Freedom: Essays on Human Existence*. Macmillan Publishers, 1955.

Heschel, Abraham Joshua. *A Passion for Truth*. Macmillan Publishers, 1973.

His Holiness, the Dalai Lama, Archbishop Desmond Tutu, with Douglas Abrams. *The Book of Joy: Lasting Happiness in a Changing World.* Avery, 2016.

Hossenfelder, Sabine. *Existential Physics: A Scientist's Guide to Life's Biggest Questions.* Viking, 2022.

Huxley, Aldous. *The Perennial Philosophy.* Harper Perennial Modern Classics, 1945, 2009.

Huxley, Aldous. *The Divine Within.* Harper Perennial Modern Classics, 1992.

James, William. *The Varieties of Religious Experience.* First Modern Library Edition, 1936.

Johnson, James Weldon. *God's Trombones: Seven Negro Sermons in Verse.* Viking Press, 1927.

Kabat-Zinn, Jon. *Full Catastrophe Living: Using the Wisdom of Your Body and Mind to Face Stress, Pain, and Illness.* Delta, 1990.

King, Martin Luther Jr. *Why We Can't Wait.* New York: New American Library, Harper & Row, 1964.

Kornfield, Jack. *A Path with Heart: A Guide through the Perils and Promises of Spiritual Life.* Bantam Books, 1993.

Kurtz, Ernest, and Ketcham, Katherine. *The Spirituality of Imperfection: Storytelling and the Search for Meaning.* Bantam Books, 1992.

Kurtz, Ernest, and Ketcham, Katherine. *Experiencing Spirituality: Finding Meaning Through Storytelling.* Jeremy P. Tarcher/Penguin, 2014.

Kushner, Harold. *When Bad things Happen to Good People.* Avon Books, 1981.

Kushner, Harold. *Who Needs God?* Pocket Books, 1989.

Lame Deer, John (Fire), and Erdoes, Richard. *Lame Deer: Seeker of Visions.* Washington Square Press, 1972, 1976, 1994.

Lamott, Anne. *Plan B: Further Thoughts on Faith.* Riverhead Books, 2005.

MacGregor, Neil. *Living with the Gods: On Beliefs and Peoples.* Alfred A. Knopf, 2018.

Marx, Karl. *"Introduction." A Contribution to the Critique of Hegel's Philosophy of Right,* translated by A. Jolin and J. O'Malley, edited by J. O'Malley. Cambridge University Press, 1843, 1970.

Matt, Daniel C. *God and the Big Bang: Discovering Harmony between Science & Spirituality.* Jewish Lights Publishing, 1996, 2016.

McCabe, Ian. *Carl Jung and Alcoholics Anonymous: The Twelve Steps as a Spiritual Journey of Individuation.* Routledge, 2018.

McGaa, Ed, Eagle Man. *Mother Earth Spirituality.* HarperOne, 1990.

McGaa, Ed, Eagle Man. *Rainbow Tribe: Ordinary People Journeying on the Red Road.* Harper San Francisco, 1992.

Merton, Thomas. *Disputed Questions.* Harcourt Brace Jovanovich, 1985.

Mishkan HaNefesh: Machzor for the Days of Awe - Rosh Hashanah. Central Conference of American Rabbis, 2015.

Mishkan Hanefesh: Machzor for the Days of Awe – Yom Kippur. Central Conference of American Rabbis, 2015.

Moon, Rev. Charles III. *Relevant Rambles: Musings of a Methodist Preacher in Recovery.* Powerful Potential & Purpose Publishing, 2021.

Morinis, Alan. *Every Day, Holy Day: 365 Days of Teachings and Practices from the Jewish Tradition of Mussar*. Trumpeter, 2010.

Mowrer, O. Hobart. *"Small Groups in Historical Perspective," in Explorations in Self-Help and Mutual Aid*. ed. Leonard D. Borman. Center for Urban Studies, Northwestern University, 1974.

Nemeck, Francis Kelly, OMI and Coombs, Marie, Hermit. *O Blessed Night: Recovering from Addiction, Codependency, and Attachment Based on the Insights of St. John of the Cross and Pierre Teilhard de Chardin*. Alba House, Society of Saint Paul, 1991.

NIV Holy Bible. Zondervan, 2011.

Richard Rohr's Daily Meditations. meditations@cac.org, *Praying with Nature*, Monday, October 30, 2023. Used by permission of cac.org.

Richard Rohr's Daily Meditations. meditations@cac.org, *We are What We See*, Monday, December 4, 2023. Used by permission of cac.org.

Richard Rohr's Daily Meditations. meditations@cac.org, *The Soul of Nature*, Sunday, March 3, 2024. Used by permission of cac.org.

Richard Rohr's Daily Meditations. meditations@cac.org, *Facing Reality to Awaken Ourselves*, Friday, March 15, 2024. Used by permission of cac.org.

Richard Rohr's Daily Meditations. meditations@cac.org, *Life in the Spirit: Weekly Summary*, Saturday, May 25, 2024. Used by permission of cac.org.

Schoen, David E. *The War of the Gods in Addiction: C.G. Jung, Alcoholics Anonymous, and Archetypal Evil*. Spring Journal Books, 2009.

Shapiro, Rami. *Recovery, the Sacred Art: The Twelve Steps as Spiritual Practice*. SkyLight Paths Publishing, 2009.

Shapiro, Rami. *Holy Rascals: Advice for Spiritual Revolutionaries*. Sounds True, Inc., 2017.

Shoemaker, Helen Smith. *I Stand by the Door: The Life of Sam Shoemaker.* Word Books, 1967.

S., Laura and Boorstein, Sylvia, 12 Steps on Buddha's Path: Bill, Buddha, and We. Reprinted by arrangement with Wisdom Publications, Inc., 2006.

Special Eurobarometer. Biotechnology, October 2010.

Special Eurobarometer, *383. Discrimination in the EU in 2012.* European Union: European Commission, 2012.

Stein, Murray. *Jung's Map of the Soul.* Open Court, 1998.

Steindl-Rast, Brother David. *99 Names of God.* Translated from the German by Peter Dahm Robertson, Orbis Books, 2021.

Steinsaltz, Adin. *The Thirteen Petalled Rose: A Discourse on the Essence of Jewish Existence & Belief.* Maggid Books, Expanded Edition, 1996.

The 14th Dalai Lama. *Our Own Heart Is the Temple.* www.justdharma. org, August 25, 2023.

Thurman, Howard. *Meditations of the Heart.* Beacon Press, 1953, 1981.

Torode, Sam. *Living from the Soul: The 7 Spiritual Principles of Ralph Waldo Emerson.* www.samtorode.com, 2020.

Tozer, A.W. *The Knowledge of the Holy, The Pursuit of God, God's Pursuit of Man, Three Spiritual Classics in One Volume.* Moody Publishers, 1948, 1950, 1961.

Twelve Steps and Twelve Traditions. Alcoholics Anonymous World Services, Inc., 1952.

https://goodreads.com/quotes/15321.Confucius.

https://www.azquotes.com/author/9220-Archibald_MacLeish.

https://www.goodreads.com/quotes- George Carlin.

https://www.episcopal.cafe/William_temple_2/.

https://libquotescom/ralph-waldo-emerson/.

https://www.goodreads.com/author/quotes/9810.Albert_Einstein.

https:// www.Goodreads.com/quotes/8199-is-god-willing-to-prevent-evil-but-not-able-then. https://www.native-languages.org/potawatomi-legends.

https://azquotes.com/author/20458-susan_jeffers. Top 25 Quotes by Susan Jeffers.

https:// www.brainyquote.com/authors/andre-gide-quotes

https://www.goodreads.com/author/quotes/9810.Albert_Einstein.

Suggested Reading

Any of the books listed in the bibliography are interesting and may be helpful in the search for a higher power. They were helpful to me. There are thousands of other books that could also be helpful, and of course I can't provide a list of thousands of books. I encourage you to engage in your own search. You may also investigate other sources such as podcasts. I have provided here a list of some books that I have in my own library. One is a book of poems. Several are historical writings about the development of Alcoholics Anonymous. Some are more philosophical, spiritual, or religious in nature. They are listed alphabetically by the author's last name. You may also have your own favorites that you return to from time to time. I think books are wonderful, and I hope you do as well.

Alcoholics Anonymous Comes of Age: A Brief History of AA. Alcoholics Anonymous World Services, Inc., 1957, 1985.

B. Mel. *New Wine: The Spiritual Roots of the Twelve Step Miracle.* Hazelden, 1991.

Borg, Marcus J. *Reading the Bible Again for the First Time: Taking the Bible Seriously but not Literally.* HarperCollins Publishers, 2001.

C. Joe. *Beyond Belief: Agnostic Musings for 12 Step Life.* Rebellion Dogs Publishing, 2013.

Carnes, Patrick. A *Gentle Path through the Twelve Steps: The Classic Guide for All People in the Process of Recovery.* Hazelden, 1993, 2012.

Charleston, Steven. *Spirit Wheel: Meditations from an Indigenous Elder.* Broadleaf Books, 2023.

Chestnut, Glenn F. *Father Ed Dowling: Bill Wilson's Sponsor.* iUniverse, 2015.

Chestnut, Glenn F. *The Higher Power of the Twelve-Step Program: For Believers & Non-Believers.* Authors Choice Press, 2001.

Cleveland, Martha, Ph.D. and G. Arlys. *The Alternative 12 Steps: A Secular Guide to Recovery.* AA Agnostica, 2014.

Covington, Stephanie S. *A Woman's Way through the Twelve Steps.* Hazelden, 1994.

Experience, Strength and Hope: Stories from the First Three Editions of Alcoholic Anonymous. Alcoholics Anonymous World Services, Inc., 2003.

Frankl, Viktor E. *Man's Search for Meaning.* Beacon Press, 2006.

Guengerich, Galen. *The Way of Gratitude: A New Spirituality for Today.* Random House, 2020.

Hammarskjold, Dag. *Markings.* Vintage Spiritual Classics, 1964, 1992, 2006.

Hirschfield, Jerry. *The Twelve Steps for Everyone…who really wants them.* Hazelden, 1975, 1977, 1987, 1990.

Hitchens, Christopher. *god is not Great: How Religion Poisons Everything.* Twelve, 2007.

Kurtz, Ernest. *Not-God: A History of Alcoholics Anonymous.* Hazelden, 1979.

Merkle, John C. *The Genesis of Faith: The Depth Theology of Abraham Joshua Heschel.* Macmillan Publishing Company, 1985.

Merton, Thomas. *No Man Is an Island.* Harcourt Brace Jovanovich, Publishers, 1955, 1983.

Merton, Thomas. *The Way of Chuang Tzu.* New Directions, 1965.

Miles, Jack. *God: A Biography.* Vintage Books, 1995.

Mitchell, Stephen, editor. *The Enlightened Heart: An Anthology of Sacred Poetry.* Harper & Row, 1989.

Mitchell, Stephen, editor. *The Enlightened Mind: An Anthology of Sacred Prose.* Harper Perennial, 1991.

Munn, Jeffrey, LMFT. *Staying Sober Without God: The Practical 12 Steps to Long-Term Recovery from Alcoholism & Addictions.* Jeffrey Munn, 2021.

Nolan, Albert. *Jesus Before Christianity.* Orbis Books, 1976, 1992, 2001.

Pass It On: The Story of Bill Wilson and How the AA Message Reached the World. Alcoholics Anonymous World Services, Inc., 1984.

Rohr, Richard. *Breathing Under Water: Spirituality and the Twelve* Steps. Franciscan Media, 2011, 2021.

Schaberg, William H. *Writing the Big Book: The Creation of AA.* Central Recovery Press, 2019.

Schrodinger, Erwin. My *View of the World.* Cambridge University Press, 1964.

Sonsino, Rifat, and Syme, Daniel B. *Finding God: Selected Responses.* UAHC Press, 2002.

Sparks, Tav. *The Wide-Open Door: The Twelve Steps, Spiritual Tradition, & the New Psychology.* Hazelden, 1993.

Taylor, Barbara Brown. *Holy Envy.* HarperOne, 2014.

The Language of the Heart: Bill W.'s Grapevine Writings. AAGrapevine, Inc., 1988.

Thomsen, Robert. *Bill W.* Harper & Row, Publishers, 1975.

Twerski, Abraham. *The Spiritual Self.* Hazelden, 2000.

Weatherhead, Leslie D. *The Christian Agnostic.* Abdington Press, 1965.

Printed in the United States
by Baker & Taylor Publisher Services